ON:

MEMOIRS OF A PRIVATE DOG TRAINER

GARY ABELOV

Published by Starry Night Publishing.Com

Rochester, New York

Copyright 2014 Gary Abelov

This book remains the copyrighted property of the author, and may not be reproduced, copied and distributed for commercial, or noncommercial purposes. Thank you for your support.

Gary Abelov

Gary Abelov

For Saykee

Gary Abelov

Contents

Gary Abelov

Prologue

Dogs, not unlike people, can develop behavior problems and find themselves in serious trouble. Some of the dogs I see are causing marital tensions, have been quarantined for biting people, and have triggered lawsuits by neighbors and even relatives.

As a dog trainer who has specialized in problem behavior for over 30 years, I see wild, unruly, often frightening dogs every day.

A typical workday for me includes a lot of driving, as I cover the entire metropolitan St. Louis area. Every day, I'll visit two or three homes and spend between one and three hours at each one. While some of the dogs I see are dangerously aggressive, most are just wonderful dogs with a few "issues."

In order to help a dog, I have to "go through" their guardians. Most of my clients are receptive to my advice, but some can be difficult to teach. Complex and difficult personalities abound, a fact which can create obvious challenges.

Many of my clients have been struggling with their dog's behavior problems for months and even years. Frequently they have paid good money to several trainers without resolving their dog's problems. All too often they are physically and emotionally exhausted and sometimes also financially drained. When they call me, they almost always say, in varied ways, that they are at the "end of my rope." Sometimes they'll tell me that they have "tried everything" and nothing seems to work. The most common thing I hear is, "Gary, I've had dogs all of my life, but I've never seen a problem like this."

And how about this for pressure? "This is her last chance. If you can't help us fix the problem, we will have to give her away or euthanize her."

In spite of the physical and emotional challenges, I love my work. I consider myself truly blessed, or very lucky, to work at something I love. I make a comfortable living and derive tremendous satisfaction from helping dogs who are in trouble.

I never intended to become a dog trainer or a behavior consultant. It seems that things just sort of evolved, and I'm really glad they did.

Meeting new dogs every day can be interesting enough, but their people are endlessly fascinating as well. I just never know what will happen when I walk into the homes and lives of these dogs and their people.

I wish I could say that I have been able to "fix" every dog that I've been employed to work with. Some dogs are so damaged, violent or out of control that my best efforts fail. I've had to accept the fact that I just can't save them all, but I do try.

The following stories are true, but names have been changed. I could go on about my approach to dog training, my philosophy and beliefs, but I have resolved to keep the introduction short and let the stories speak for themselves.

Eddie Spaghetti

The shelter director asked if I'd be interested in helping them with their dogs. They were a "no kill" sanctuary that was home to nearly 400 cats and 125 dogs. Some of those dogs needed some behavioral help. Many more were in need of training.

There were leash problems by the dozen. Others were just wild and confused. Most were there through no fault of their own. Divorce, death. People losing their jobs or their homes. Many of them, of course, were strays. I walked through the kennels with the kennel manager, asking questions about each dog and taking notes on every dog. I noted their breed, gender, how long they had been at the shelter, behavior problems, etc.

Diane, the kennel manager, had a meeting to attend, so I continued my tour of the kennel myself. At the next to the last run, I saw him. He was sitting on his bed with perhaps the saddest, most dejected look on his face that I had ever seen on a dog. I looked at the card on his gate. It just said, "Eddie." As I turned to look at him, our eyes met for a few seconds before I turned to gaze at his body. He was skinny but not emaciated. As I looked back at his face, I could see that his lower jaw was sharply angulated. It was not symmetrical. His deformity looked as if his jaw had been broken and had never set properly. Or maybe he was born that way. I didn't know. I couldn't help but wonder how he'd ended up here. He was an obviously sad and lonely little guy who looked like he didn't have a friend in the world.

"Hi Eddie. Would you like a treat?" I slowly sat down on the floor beside his bed. His tail wagged slowly. He took the cookie from my hand and made fast work of it. I offered another. "Here, Eddie. Try this," I said as I handed him a piece of a hot dog. Boy he loved that! He stood up and, tail wagging, looked at me as if to say, "Got any more?"

I handed him the rest of the hotdog, and while he was chewing it, I began to rub his chest with the back of my hand. He moved closer. "Hey Eddie, wanna be friends?" He moved even closer and wanted to smell my ear, then the side of my face and finally the top of my head. I took a long look at Eddie's face again. I just had never seen a dog like this. I really felt sorry for him, the way a person might feel sorry when encountering a terribly disfigured person on the street. Maybe someone abandoned him because of his appearance. The longer I looked at him, the more I was drawn to him. Eddie was a special dog. I wasn't sure why, but I could feel "something" being around him. I would soon find out that I was the only one that felt that way. No one at the shelter seemed to like Eddie. The kennel staff talked about him like he was radioactive. "What do you know about Eddie?" I would ask. The answer was usually, "Not much. He's afraid of everything." Some would add, "He sure is ugly!"

Later on that day I returned to Eddie's run to take him for a walk. When I approached him, he had the same downcast look on his face that he had earlier that afternoon. "Hey Eddie," I said, as I opened the gate to his enclosure. "Wanna go for a walk, buddy?" His tail wagged back and forth. I petted him a bit and slipped a lead over his head.

As we approached the exit of the kennel, I could see that he was more than hesitant. He was afraid. I opened the door and tried to reassure him, being careful not to pull on his neck. "C'mon old buddy. Let's go outside." We took about eight or ten steps across the parking lot and Eddie frantically began pulling me towards a tiny little plant growing on the right side of the lot. He was actually attempting to hide under the plant! I encouraged Eddie to walk with me towards the office at the opposite end of the parking area, where we both sat down on a patch of grass under a shady Oak tree. As I petted Eddie, he moved in closer, eventually standing on my lap. After a few minutes he lay across my lap and placed his head under my right arm. We spent some time like that, Eddie and I. I spoke softly to him and stroked his head and back. Had it not been for his severely deformed jaw, he would be a handsome dog.

Looking at his teeth, I guessed him to be about a year and a half old. He was medium sized and was a mix of Shar Pei and God only knows what else. The little guy was growing on me quickly. As we sat there getting to know one another, we watched people come and go from the shelter's administrative office. A couple of the kennel workers walked by with leashed dogs. I could see them checking out Eddie and me. I think they were probably wondering what I was doing with "that ugly dog."

The following day, I hurried through my other duties at the shelter. I was anxious to see Eddie. When I brought him out of the kennel, he once again pulled me with all his strength toward the little plant and tried to "hide" under it. The plant was about two feet tall, a young rose bush actually. It had no blooms on it, so it was at the most four inches wide. With some coaxing, Eddie got up and followed me back to the shady Oak tree where we sat down just like we had the day before. As I was petting him, I said, "Eddie, Eddie. Eddie Spaghetti." It became his new name. As the kennel people and volunteers walked by, they asked what I thought of Eddie. "You mean Eddie Spaghetti?" I'd answer. I love him! What a great dog!"

The following afternoon I began taking Eddie on long walks on the country lane that winds around behind the shelter. I couldn't help but notice that Eddie didn't pull me towards the little rose bush this time. As we returned from our walk, a volunteer said, smiling, "Eddie! Eddie Spaghetti!" Eddie looked at her and wagged his tail. He seemed pleased that somebody was greeting him.

I didn't see Eddie for a few days after that. We resumed our walks through the country, and I began to see a big, big change in Eddie. His confidence was really growing. He no longer seemed afraid of people and where he once was terrified of cars, now I was taking him for rides in my truck. I was amazed how quickly he was coming out of his shell. Equally amazing was the changes in the shelter staffs' attitude towards Eddie. At one time, they avoided Eddie like the plague. Now volunteers and staff were always petting him affectionately. As the weeks went by, everyone began calling him Eddie Spaghetti. It was miraculous. It was as if everyone suddenly decided it was ok to like the ugly dog.

I was worried that in spite of all these positive changes, Eddie's deformity would prevent him from ever becoming adopted. I tried to put that thought out of my mind, but it would come back again and again as I continued to love on him and work with him. I taught Eddie to sit and lie down. He even learned how to "high five." More weeks went by. The kennel staff had, much to my surprise and amazement, made a 100 per cent change in their attitude towards Eddie. They too had fallen for him, and Eddie responded. The once depressed, lonely little dog had transformed himself into a happy-go-lucky love machine. Everybody became his friend. He became a celebrity of sorts around the shelter. Whenever Eddie was out and about, people would usually chant "Eddie Spaghetti. Eddie Spaghetti!" Eddie's face would just light up. He at times would look up at me and make sure I noticed. "See how much everyone likes me."

One day the shelter held an adoption event. All day long, dogs and cats were being adopted. It was a happy affair. Staff and volunteers live to see furry kids find homes. Yet with all the adoptions taking place, nobody would even look at Eddie. I had given him a bath myself that morning. I even decked him out in a yellow bandana. He looked wonderful, but nobody gave him more than a quick glance. Nobody could see past his deformity. "I guess he'll be a lifer at the shelter," I thought sadly.

Suddenly a young family stopped to look at Eddie. I watched from a distance as the kids knelt down to pet Eddie, who responded by happily licking their faces. The little boy hugged him. Then his sister hugged him.

I walked towards Eddie, but he didn't see me. He was far too busy eating up the love he was getting from mom, dad and the kids. I didn't want to interfere. Everyone was smiling and talking about Eddie. This family had found their perfect dog. They had fallen in love with and soon adopted Eddie Spaghetti.

Tiki

Tiki was my first small dog. I was just getting started with my dog training career and had yet only worked with large dogs. I'd never even lived with a small dog, but I knew I'd need some small dog experience eventually.

At the time I was busy building my business. My friend Diana has designed my first business card. A talented artist, Diana needed only an hour to come up with the design and the simple phrase: Dog Training by Gary Abelov. I tacked the cards on bulletin boards and in veterinary offices all over St. Louis. I also placed an ad in a local newspaper called The Riverfront Times.

Gradually, the calls began. Some just wanted regular dog training. Others had dogs with behavior problems. With each new client, I gained confidence in my ability to train and diagnose problems.

I was still struggling financially, so I was happy when I received the call from a woman in Kirkwood, a St. Louis suburb. "I'd like you to train my Chihuahua mix, Tiki," she said. By then I'd helped people train 15 dogs, but I had zero experience with a Chihuahua-sized dog. What if Tiki didn't excel? I was still young and green, but I needed to work with a little dog sooner or later. There was no turning back. Tiki's owner and I agreed I would take Tiki through a series of lessons.

When I arrived at Tiki's home, her guardian, Liz, met be outside the home and never did invite me inside. She was a pleasant-looking middle-aged woman, but the first thing I noticed was her black eye. Trying not to stare, I explained my approach to training. She then handed me a leash which was attached to a small dog. "This is Tiki," she said with a smile. "Knock if you need anything." She went inside, leaving me alone with Tiki.

OK. It was a nice day. I didn't mind staying in the front lawn. I soon learned Tiki was brilliant. I was shocked. Tiki was also adorable and sweet. I loved teaching her basic commands and found working with such an intelligent dog exciting.

By the end of the third lesson, I was smitten. What a sweetheart! At each level of training, Tiki excelled.

Every time I returned to Liz's house, Tiki would be watching me from the living room window. She'd run to the front door and jump up and down, crying and barking with happiness. Liz and I would always stand outside the door for a few minutes and talk about Tiki's progress. As my lessons continued, her black eye faded.

My arrangement with Liz was not typical. Usually my clients paid for hourly "obedience" lessons. After each class, I asked that the client practice with the dog during the week and call me if and when they wanted to go on. But Liz wanted me to train her dog myself. As a result, I visited her home often. We agreed on 15 lessons at a cost of $175, which seemed pretty grand in 1984 when I was broke most of the time.

Since Tiki was going to be my first "graduate," I realized I needed a graduation certificate, so I had some certificates printed.

After a few lessons, Tiki and I became very close. Best pals even. Lesson after lesson, Tiki performed magnificently. That sweet little girl taught me that a dog that was small in stature could still have a huge personality and a keen mind. I was thoroughly enjoying my new career, and I was proud of myself. After all, I was making money doing what I loved and now I had a bright little dog about to graduate.

The weeks flew by, and it was time for our last lesson. I was in a great mood. But when I arrived at Tiki's home, Liz was not happy. I could see that she had been crying. "Are you alright?" I asked as Tiki pushed her way past Liz and sat in front of me, tail wagging vigorously. As I knelt down to pet Tiki, Liz said, "Gary, I don't know if this is Tiki's last lesson; I've lost track. But it doesn't matter, you can't come back here anymore."

Liz started crying again and through her tears, she said, "My husband doesn't want you to come here. He is very jealous. I'm so sorry."

I was stunned and shocked by what she had just said. More than that, I was speechless and hurt. I had been completely professional. How could her husband be jealous? I was also a little upset to think I would never see Tiki again.

As Liz urged me to hurry away before her husband came home, I picked up Tiki and did something I had never done before. I gave her a long hug and kissed her on the top of her head. "Bye Liz. Bye Tiki," I said quietly as I put Tiki down.

I walked back to my truck, hopped in and began to back out of the driveway when a white delivery-type van pulling up quickly behind me, blocking my exit. The van's driver jumped from his vehicle and charged towards my truck. From the look on his face, I knew I was about to encounter Liz's angry, jealous husband. He obviously wanted to talk, so I somewhat reluctantly rolled down the window.

"I don't appreciate your hanging out with my wife," he yelled. I felt like checking to see if there was anyone standing behind me. Me?

"What are you talking about?" I returned.

"I know you are sleeping with her," he growled.

I replied, "Look, you are wrong, just plain wrong. I've never even set foot in your house. All I've done is train your dog." *Try not to act nervous. Try not to act nervous,* I told myself.

He just stood there, staring at me, before he finally left and backed his van out of my path. As a backed out, I looked back at the house and saw Tiki looking out the window.

I barely knew what to think. Should I be flattered that I'd been threatened by a jealous husband? Would other guys be impressed with my story?

Or should I be rethinking my career? Dog training is more dangerous than I originally thought.

In the end, I just felt sad and sorry for Liz. I now understood her black eye. This was my first exposure to "domestic violence" and I didn't like what I saw.

Tiki never did get her graduation certificate, but to this day I think about her though I know she must have passed on long ago. I have worked with countless little dogs since Tiki, but she was my first and she was a special little lady.

Are You a Dog Whisperer?

In the late '90s, a cool movie called The Horse Whisperer came out. It starred Robert Redford who played a quiet, intelligent, horse trainer. I liked the film's primary message that you can rehabilitate animals with compassion and patience. A few months after the movie's release, someone asked me if I was a "dog whisperer." I was asked that question literally hundreds of times over the new few years.

I explained to everyone that I wasn't a dog whisperer. The name implied that I had a special gift that enabled me to speak to animals in a secret language and that I could somehow magically turn around any dog in the world. I knew "my stuff" where dogs were concerned. I had a good understanding of dog psychology, breeds of dogs, etc., but I wasn't a magician or a dog whisperer. I didn't want people to think I would sort everything out for them after a brief and very quiet chat with their dog. I'd spent years teaching people that with a little knowledge and guidance, THEY could turn their dog's behavior around. In time the term "dog whisperer" began to fade and away, and I was glad to see it go.

My relief ended abruptly when The National Geographic Channel introduced a new program featuring Cesar Milan and titled, you guessed it, "The Dog Whisperer." At first I enjoyed the show since it was set in California, state of my boyhood. I loved seeing palm trees and the ocean, and I liked seeing another trainer making house calls and emphasizing exercise and training for dogs. Unfortunately, my interest in the show began to wane when Cesar began talking about "pack leaders" and becoming the "alpha." These catchy names and phrases are really not based on sound wolf biology and, quite frankly, wolves and domestic dogs have very little in common.

Canis Lupus (the wolf) and Canis Familiaris (the modern dog) may be distant relatives, but DNA studies indicate approximately 30,000 to 50,000 years of domestication between the wolf and the dog. Dogs simply can't do what wolves do and vice versa. Furthermore, even in a wolf pack there is no single "pack leader." Sorry Cesar.

Wolf biologists stopped using the name "alpha" more than 20 years ago. They now talk about the breeding pair as having the authority to direct the pack on a daily basis. In fact, the female in the breeding pair carries as much authority as the male and much more when it comes to the den and her puppies. So the myth that there is a single, male "dominant" wolf in the pack is just plain wrong. There is no pounding down of the subordinates as many people wrongfully believe.

Wolves form extremely intelligent, close knit family units. They rarely if ever fight among themselves. They cannot risk injury to themselves or to others in the pack. They depend on each other for hunting and for their very survival.

The idea that if you don't become the "alpha" in your relationship to your dog, your dog will try to become your "alpha" is simply absurd. Dogs need love, education, and parental leadership. What they don't need, want or understand is a person who becomes physical with them to prove he/she is the "alpha." The resulting tension can completely destroy the relationship between a dog and his human companion.

Treat your dog with respect. Train him/her with love, and you will have a loyal friend for life. Learn about wolves. They are one of the most fascinating animals in the world. But take the old "alpha" theory, place it in a missile, and blast it into outer space where it belongs.

Bad Ass Bear

Through West St. Louis County winds a scenic two-lane road named Wild Horse Creek Road. In the '70s and early '80s, Wild Horse turned from a quiet, lonely country road with just a spattering of old farmhouses to an area of subdivisions with multi-million dollar homes. Affluent horse owners were among those who discovered the area and established horse farms.

Wild Horse Creek Road always reminded me of Mulholland Drive in Los Angeles. Mulholland runs along the spine of the Santa Monica Mountains, separating the San Fernando Valley from Beverly Hills, Westwood, and Pacific Palisades. As a kid I loved riding my trusty 10-speed Schwinn along this route. The views along Mulholland were awesome, and the road has been depicted in countless motion pictures. Both Wild Horse Creek Road and Mulholland have long been considered great places to park and make out.

Bicyclists and motorcyclists loved both of these roads, as did people cruising in their top down convertibles. And in West St. Louis County, Bad Ass Bear, a two-year-old Rottweiler, loved chasing bicyclists and motorcyclists along Wild Horse Creek Road. And that was one of the reasons why I found myself one day at the home of his family, a couple recently resettled here from San Diego along with their 10 adopted children. They'd adopted Bear for the children. Now they were in trouble.

"He is becoming increasingly aggressive and territorial. Do you think you can help him?"

Bear's owners were one of those with a horse ranch, an expansive place with horses grazing in the pasture, a new barn, a circular drive, and surrounding it all, a white fence. The entire family greeted me and we talked inside while Bear remained outside in his kennel.

"Gary, Mister Bad Ass Bear has been chasing everyone down Wild Horse Creek Road. He doesn't go after cars, just guys on Harleys and bicycles," mom said.

She explained that Bear hadn't actually bitten anyone, "but he'd come close." People had reported him and the police had paid a couple visits. "If we see him, we call him back to us. Sometimes he listens to us and gives up the chase, but sometimes he doesn't."

I began with a few basic questions.

"Is Bear neutered?"

"No."

"Has Bear had any training?"

"Not really, but he can sit on command and shake his paw."

Where does Bear sleep?"

"Wherever he wants."

"What does he eat? How much exercise does he get? And so on.

After I finished with the basic information, I asked mom to bring Bear into the room. They were worried about how he might act around me, which caused me a little concern. OK. Maybe more than a little. I asked that Bear be wearing a collar (not prong or choke) that he cannot back out of and that the person bringing him in be able to hold him back if he rushed towards me. I hadn't seen Bear yet, but as mom opened the door to the yard, I saw....HOLY COW! He's a big one! ~~Maybe~~ 120 lbs. or more, I thought, than mom him weighed. Bear was also ~~all~~ muscle. ~~Gigantic! Seriously huge!~~

In the next seconds Bear escaped from mom and raced straight across the room, dove under the table and came up between my legs, teeth barred and growling. I feared I was about to lose my testicles and maybe my life, which now flashed before ~~me.~~ my eyes.

With what consciousness I still had, I turned my head to the side, a "calming signal used universally by dogs which means, "I mean no harm. I don't want any trouble." Meanwhile, mom says, "C'mon Bear. Let's go for a ride. Wanna go for a walk?" Bingo! Bear backs out from under the table and happily allows her to attach his leash. She puts Bear outside and I realize I haven't taken a breath in a long time.

So, back to work. First, I advised the family that it would be a good idea to neuter Bear as soon as possible. I also suggested the use of an invisible fence around the back of the house so Bear could go outside but would be kept away from Wild Horse Creek Road. Then he needed some serious training to help him develop some much needed respect and self-control. I met with Bear's family several more times until I felt we had Bear's behavior under control.

Much to everyone's relief, Bear turned out to be a willing student. The bicyclists and motorcyclists on Wild Horse Creek Road no longer needed to watch out for Bear.

But I will never forget the feeling of impending doom as Bear ran towards me and showed me his teeth while between my legs.

Bad Ass Bear, you definitely took a few years off my life.

Gary Abelov

Things that Make Me Crazy

- Clients that are not home when I arrive for an appointment.

- Clients that cancel at the last minute, sometimes while I'm on my way to their house.

- Clients that constantly look at their cell phone with I'm trying to teach them. Some even text while I'm talking with them.

- Moms who struggle to listen to me while trying to calm whining toddlers and crying infants.

- Having to repeat an entire consultation with husbands, wives, girlfriends and boyfriends who arrive an hour late.

- Dog guardians who never stop talking long enough to let me speak.

- People who start a phone conversations with "I'm on disability" or "I live on a fixed income."

- People who start our conversation with "If you can't help us, we will have to get rid of him."

- Fabulously wealthy clients who ask at the end of the consultation, "Will you bill me?"

- And the "king daddy of them all…the one that really makes me crazy
- Are you like Cesar Milan?" Or "Are you like the dog whisperer on TV?"

Gary Abelov

Loki

"Hi, Mr. Abelov. I have an Akita female about a year old that I need some help with.

"She is very hard to walk; she jumped on me yesterday, and for the first time, growled at me. Do you think you could come out and work with her?"

We talked for a while and then he said, "By the way, this is my son's dog, and to be honest with you, my son is in prison. My son loves Loki. It's all he talks about in his letters and phone calls. I hope we can get his dog straightened out before he gets out in six weeks."

We agreed to meet the following week. To this point, everything seemed pretty straight forward. I certainly didn't foresee any problems. I would soon learn otherwise.

I arrived early at my appointment so I spend some time straightening up the front of my car while observing the ranch-style home and its large, expansive yard. I noticed that everything was well-cared for. To the left of the house I noticed a six-foot chain link kennel with a dog house inside and the dog I'd come to help. Loki the Akita stood in the kennel quietly watching me as I got out of the car and walked to the house. Before I could ring the doorbell, Gene opened the door to invite me in. "Hi Gary. Thanks for coming out. Are you ready to meet Loki?

"You bet, " I reply, and the two of us walk across the lawn to Loki's kennel Loki seems happy to see Gene – no barking or jumping, just some tail wagging. Gary attaches the leash to Loki's collar and I ask if I can walk her into the house. Loki was a champion puller. She pulled so hard that we were almost running. I laughed, "My goodness. You're right she's strong. She can really pull."

Once inside I asked more questions about Loki's history while noticing that Loki never took her eyes off me. That might have concerned me if I hadn't still been young and relatively new to dog training. Gene told me more about Loki's sad history.

"I love my son, but he's been in trouble off and on since he was 12 years old. He says he loves Loki, but he's very impatient, and I've seen him lose his temper and really beat her. Gene talked for about 20 minutes, telling one story after another about the abuse Loki had suffered. Then I suggested we'd start work on the pulling problem by exchanging Loki's choke collar for a head halter, which makes it easier for the walker to control the dog's head. Since the head is connected to the body, the walker gains control of the dog's entire body. The halter causes no pain and is easy to use.

Before we started, Gene excused himself to use the restroom, leaving me alone with Loki. I searched through my supplies for a large head collar while Loki sat directly in front of me. Then I got off the chair slowly and kneeling on one knee, I spoke to Loki softly. "Hi girl. You're sure pretty. Can I pet you?" I rubbed her chest softly with the back of my hand, being careful not to stare at her. She seemed receptive, so I picked up the head collar and looked towards her.

Then I saw her look directly into my eyes for the first time. It wasn't a soft look. It was a hard stare. I knew that when a dog gives you a look like that it is time to back off. But before I could do anything, Loki sprang forward with her mouth open and bit the left side of my forehead, the sudden force pushing me onto by back and throwing my glasses off my head. Loki was now on top of me, biting me over and over again—first my shoulder, then my lower stomach. I put my hand up to push her off and she chomped down hard on my hand. All of this took place in about 20 seconds. As I was fighting off Loki, Gene rushed back in the room and yelled, "Loki, Loki, No!" Gene grabbed Loki's collar and pulled her off me.

This consultation took place early in my career, and I've learned from the mistakes I made that day. I wrongly assumed that I really didn't have to watch a one year old female that carefully. I also didn't pay careful enough attention to the fact that Loki had recently growled at Gene. I had planned on discussing that later on in the session AFTER we had walked Loki.

Gene put Loki back in her kennel as I surveyed the damage to my body. There were five bites that would all require medical attention. Gene drove me to the emergency room where I arrived bent over and holding a washcloth to my forehead. That evening I spoke with Gene by phone and we agreed to meet again that weekend. By then St. Louis County Animal Control had been by to put Loki under an in-house 10-day quarantine. Physicians are required to report dog bites.

I wasn't optimistic about Loki's prospects, and I was honest with Gene. I told him that ordinarily I would continue to work with Loki but several things stood in the way. For one thing, his son, who was probably the cause of Loki's problems, was coming home soon. We both knew that the son would not cooperate with Loki's training. "He doesn't take instruction well. He thinks he knows everything," Gene admitted.

"Gene, I have tried to rehabilitate dogs for most of my adult life. So it's hard for me to say this. But if Loki was able to do this to me, a six foot two 205 lb. man, think what he could do to an unsuspecting child. (Gene had two grandchildren). You need to seriously consider putting Loki down. Your son is coming home in a few weeks. He's going to undo everything positive that we might accomplish. Loki is a true disaster waiting to happen."

Gene was sad, tearful, but understanding. He loved Loki and also didn't know what he'd tell his son. We finally agreed that a white lie might be in order. He could tell his son that someone had stolen Loki. To me, he said, "I feel like my heart is breaking."

That might have been the end of it. But strange things do happen, and Loki got a second chance after Gene's son got into a prison fight and lost any possibility of coming home for many years. Gene now wanted to continue Loki's training.

I insisted on several conditions. First, Loki must not be trusted around Gene's grandchildren. She must be kenneled whenever the grandchildren or any other visitors were around. The kennel gate must be closed with a chain and a padlock. No exceptions. Next I wanted Loki to undergo a thorough physical examination with a complete blood profile. Lastly, I wanted Gene to discuss with his veterinarian the possibility of using a psychotropic medication for Loki.

Loki's veterinarian conducted a careful exam with Loki wearing a basket muzzle and feeling groggy after a large dose of acepromazine. The vet found no physical reason to explain Loki's aggression but suggested that Fluoxetine (Prozac) might be helpful in "switching" off the anxiety in Loki's brain. With the medication and behavior modification, I hoped Loki could relearn appropriate social behavior around humans.

I'm not going to pretend that I wasn't nervous around Loki for a long time. I handled her carefully and always watched for telltale aggressive body language. I worked with Loki an hour or so a day, four times a week for nearly three months. In addition to confidence building, "obedience" training, Loki and I went hiking and even on two or three occasions went swimming. I took Loki downtown where, wearing a head collar and a basket muzzle, she was exposed to throngs of people on the sidewalks. She routinely walked by construction zones, sidewalk grates, street musicians, hot dog venders and homeless beggars. Loki would take a dip in big fountains and walk through revolving glass doors. We even hopped on an escalator. By week eight, the medicine, training, trust exercises and aerobic activity seemed to be working. The beatings she'd suffered at the hands of Gene's son now seemed to belong to a forgotten past.

Our progress wasn't always straight forward; there were times Loki would eye me suspiciously. A time or two she freaked out at the sight of strange-looking people. The second week I worked with her she growled at me when I rubbed her too vigorously. That was just enough to scare the holy shit out of me. But by week nine we were ready to work without the muzzle. Loki was no longer acting aggressively. The medicine had now taken full effect as well. Little things that had always troubled Loki – UPS trucks, riding mowers, loud motorcycles – didn't elicit so much as a yawn now. We were making genuine progress. I was still cautious with her, but I was no longer nervous.

While I was working with Loki, Gene had a six-foot red cedar fence built to enclose his entire back yard. He also installed a special lockset on the new fence's gate.

Gene and I next began taking Loki to private agility lessons twice a week. This accomplished two things. It gave Loki another outlet for her high energy, and it provided her with some confidence-building mental stimulation. I think most dog people would be surprised to see an Akita participating in Agility. We brought Loki into Agility not to compete but to teach her to use her mind. Akitas are not brilliant dogs. They possess average intelligence. Typically, you see Border Collies, Australian Shepherds, German Shepherds and a few of the more intelligent dog breeds in Agility classes. But Loki – smart or not – loved learning to leap over the hurdles, weave through poles and run through tunnels. Eventually Gene purchased some agility equipment and set it up in his backyard.

After three months of working with Loki, I was struck by the changes in her. She was now a happy, sweet, content dog. I was very proud of her progress. I was no longer on "caution overload" when I interacted with her. We had become close friends. Hell, we sometimes wrestled with one another in Gene's yard. But in spite of all the tremendous changes in Loki, Gene's daughter remained very skeptical. She insisted that Loki continue to remain outside in the yard when her children visited their grandpa.

Six months later I called Gene to see how things were progressing.

"She is doing wonderfully, Gary. Even my daughter has begun to trust Loki."

Gene said he still muzzled Loki around company but could imagine the day would come when that would not be necessary. In the meantime, he took Loki on long walks with his daughter and the grandkids, Loki still wearing her muzzle, of course.

I stayed in touch with Gene for several years. He would send me Christmas cards with pictures of Loki. Sometimes out of the blue he would call. We became pretty good friends, but I never asked him about his son, and he never mentioned him either.

Loki continued to blossom, and never again showed any aggression. I visited Loki now and then. She always remembered me and would give me a huge greeting.

Loki died at 10 years of age from bone cancer. I've worked with countless aggressive dogs since Loki. From her I learned to exercise caution at all times, to listen more carefully to my clients and definitely to be careful when fitting head collars and attaching leashes.

I continue to learn from every dog I meet. Some lessons are just a little harder (and more painful) to learn than others.

Unfortunately, my experience has been that not all violent dogs can be rehabilitated. Some owners of aggressive dogs have physical disabilities or limitations that can prevent them from stopping dog fights and attacks on people. All too often aggressive dogs are living with multiple children who cannot defend themselves or read a dog's signals. In addition, people have time restraints and emotional problems of their own to contend with. Often, my clients are under tremendous pressure from their spouse, parents and even neighbors to "get rid of the dog." Turning around an aggressive dog requires complete support from everyone who lives with the dog.

Breed characteristics, life experience, and biting history all can contribute to or detract from a successful rehabilitation.

My advice to anyone with an aggressive dog is this: Get professional help. Find a trainer or behavior consultant with appropriate experience and credentials. Avoid anyone who uses force, shock collars, or "dominance" style training. Consult with your veterinarian as well. A complete physical including a blood profile is advisable to rule out any underlying physical problems.

Unfortunately, even with the best professional help in the world, some dogs may actually not improve behaviorally. In some instances, and in spite of your best efforts, they can actually get worse. All you can do is get the best help you can find and hope for the best.

Tired Kids and Spider Monkeys

Many years ago I read a wonderful book titled Blue Highways by William Least Heat Moon. It was an autobiographic account of how Moon had his wife stolen by his best friend and lost his teaching job at the university. He decided to buy a plain delivery van, built a bed into it and traveled the back roads (blue highways) of America.

He enjoyed stopping at cafes and restaurants as he drove each day. Moon said he enjoyed the break in his solitude when he stopped to eat. He would sometimes chat with the other diners and, of course, some of the waitresses.

I could easily relate. I spend a lot of time on the road driving around St. Louis, and I love eating out. Yes, it's expensive, but it provides me with a nice distraction from my work and a full belly between clients.

Moon judged the quality of a café by how many calendars hung on the eatery's walls. If it had no calendars, the food would be edible but just barely. Two calendars meant the food was a little tasty, but nothing memorable. And so on he went, sharing that a five calendar café was the best of the best. He rarely encountered a five calendar place, but he assured us these places really did exist. He would avoid any place that advertised "Family Restaurant," expecting the food would be lousy. Likewise, he stayed away from restaurants with cute names like Kounty Klassic Kitchen" or "Aunt Mabel's Pancake House." He insisted these places were always losers when it came to cuisine.

In over 30 years of dining out, I have never once encountered a five calendar café. The most I have seen is three calendars, but I'm still hopeful.

 In visiting client's homes, I have a rating system of my own: the garage door system. No garage means the client will pay with cash. One car garage, they will always ask, "Do you prefer cash or check. A two-car garage home means I'll be paid with a check. No questions asked.

Three doors means the client will ask if I take plastic. Those with four doors never want to pay me that day. They want me to send them a bill. Sometimes they'll look for their checkbook but just can't find it. Then they'll apologize and promise to send me a check. Sometimes the check never comes. I have to call them, which I hate, to collect. I rarely get a rubber check, but when I do it's almost never from a struggling young family or a college student. It's nearly always from someone who lives in a big, beautiful home. Crazy, huh?

Dog trainers walk into the homes and lives of complete strangers. Consultations and training sessions are often interrupted by any of the following:

- Text messages
- Phone calls
- Repairmen of all types
- UPS drivers
- Neighbors
- Obnoxious, tired and hungry children
- Relatives
- Ex wives and husbands dropping off or picking up children
- Smart phones. In addition to the calls that must be answered, I often see clients trying discreetly to text or check emails while I'm talking to them.

But the interruptions in homes pale compared to the interruptions when working with people at their businesses. I've conducted training at car dealerships, beauty shops, taxidermy studio, antique store, nursing homes, dress shop, apartment building roof, spa, boarding stable, bird supply store, attorney's office, school gymnasium and television studio.

I once tried to conduct a behavioral consultation in a basement in South St. Louis. The woman was a hairstylist who was actually washing someone's hair while we were talking about her dog. When she finished the shampoo, I followed her over to the woman who was having her hair cut. When she finished with her clients, we resumed our consultation upstairs in her apartment above the salon.

As I sat down on her couch, her pet spider monkey ran up to me, jumped on my head and bit the top of my ear. Was my client concerned? Oh hell no. She thought it was hilarious.

Gary Abelov

Walk Across Missouri

I began learning about puppy mills in the late seventies. The more I read about them, the more horrified I became. "How could such places exit?" I wondered. Could there really be thousands of these places around the country? How could anyone be so greedy and so cruel that they could operate these terrible puppy farms?

As my research progressed, I learned more:

Missouri earned the title, "Puppy Mill Capital of the U.S.A."

The dogs in these almost always cramped, filthy places are bred on every heat cycle.

Almost all pet store puppies come from puppy mills.

The economic impact on a puppy mill community can be staggering when officials close down these places. Veterinary care and boarding can range from $100,000 to as high as $500,000.

The environmental impact from puppy mills can be devastating to the community in which they exist. The pathogens from dog feces can be swept into streams and rivers that are also sources of public drinking water and recreation. In the case of one West Virginia puppy farm, the coliform bacteria load on a local stream was 400 times greater than the legal limit.

According to the American Society for Prevention of Cruelty to Animals (ASPCA), a puppy mill is "a large scale commercial dog breeding operation where profit is given priority over the wellbeing of the dogs. Unlike responsible breeders who place the utmost importance on producing the healthiest puppies possible, breeding at puppy mills is performed without consideration of genetic quality. This results in generations of dogs with unchecked hereditary defects."

How many puppies come from the mills? According to the Better Business Bureau and the Humane Society of the United States, 2.04 million puppies come from USDA licensed breeding facilities. According to 2014 figures, most of these facilities are located in Missouri, Kansas, Ohio, Iowa, Oklahoma, Pennsylvanian and Arkansas.

And Missouri has by far the largest number of "Class A" dog breeding facilities at 558. Iowa is next with 208. Arkansas has 132, Ohio 162, Oklahoma 165, Kansas 148, and Pennsylvania 99.

I learned that the largest wholesaler of puppies, the Hunte Corporation, is located in Goodman, MO. In 2007 alone, Hunte sold 96,000 puppies and pulled in $20 million in sales. A few other fun facts about Hunte: The Better Business Bureau (BBB) give Hunte an "F" rating. Hunte has received millions of dollars in loans from the United States Department of Agriculture (USDA) to help expand their business. The ASPCA says Missouri puppy mills generate revenue of over $40 million annually.

Kathleen Summers of the HSUS Puppy Mill Task Force says, "Many Missouri puppy mill owners are repeat offenders and have dropped their USDA licenses to avoid Federal scrutiny but are still licensed by the Missouri Department of Agriculture. This way they can still sell sick, abused animals.

I am especially concerned that we still have too many unlicensed dog breeding operations existing without any state or federal oversight. Hundreds of thousands of dogs continue to suffer from neglect. The HSUS says, "The current gaping loophole in the Animal Welfare Act regulations is the exclusion of certain "retail" pet sellers from federal oversight. When deplorable facilities are finally closed down, local agencies, non-profits and municipal governments are often saddled with the expense of cleaning up, removing the dogs and handling judicial costs.

Year after year, I visit the homes of the people who have purchased or rescued puppy mill dogs. It's heartbreaking and frustrating. It's always amazing and almost miraculous when I see puppies that have escaped from the mills physically and psychologically unscathed. The most common problem that I am called to help with is fear. The eighth week of a dog's life is known as "the critical fear imprinting time." If a puppy is not exposed to a variety of people during this time (and up to the 16th week), they will most likely view social interaction with strangers as something to avoid. Likewise, dogs who are held in cages during this critical development period and are not exposed to a variety of differing geographic locations will find most novel experiences frightening.

I won't spend a lot of time here attempting to describe the concentration camp like conditions in many of these places. I'm sure most of you already know about them. Living in tiny cages, these dogs are rarely socialized with people. The adult dogs at the mills are not "played with." They are considered "units" in the jargon of the commercial dog breeding industry.

All too often the dogs in puppy mills rarely if ever receive medical attention. As a result, they suffer from deafness, respiratory disorders, kidney diseases, hip/elbow dysplasia, and luxating patellas. They often suffer from heart disease and epilepsy. And let's not forget giardia. A dog from a puppy mill might come home with distemper, parvo virus, mange, heartworms, kennel cough, ticks and fleas, chronic diarrhea and a whole host of internal parasites.

Following are a few details from the 2012 HS Institute for Science and Policy "Animal Studies Report":

When 80 dogs were rescued from a puppy mill in North Carolina, a veterinarian with the local SPCA reported that 50% of the dogs were afflicted with parasites, 23% suffered from various serious eye disorders, all of the dogs over 18 months of age showed evidence of moderate to severe periodontal disease. One of the dogs had such severe dental disease that she required 32 dental extractions, while others had periodontal disease so severe that it led to bone resorption of the mandible (eroded jaw bone). Six dogs suffered from pyoderma (skin disease) caused by urine soaked, matted fur.

When authorities removed more than 100 dogs from a puppy mill in Stuarts Draft, VA, in August 2009, a 200 page veterinarian report indicated that out of 80 dogs examined, more than 50% of them suffered from a disorder serious enough for them to require emergency veterinary care. More than 80% suffered from parasites, 40% were underweight, more than 35% suffered from dehydration.

Confinement and deprivation can have long-term physical and psychological ramifications.

Dr. Frank McMillan, DVM, of the University of Pennsylvania School of Medicine studied more than 1,100 former puppy mill dogs who had been in their new homes an average of two years. Details from his research appeared in USA Today (October 10, 2011).

Dr. McMillan found that the former puppy mill dogs showed significantly elevated levels of fears and phobias, compulsive and repetitive behaviors, and heightened sensitivity to being touched compared to "normal" pet dogs. They were six to eight times more likely to score in the highest ranges of fear.

Because I am a Behavior Consultant and because I live in St. Louis, Missouri, puppy mills are of great concern to me. Please, make no mistake. It is no accident that puppy mills thrive in Missouri, where the conservative rural population hates any "government interference." Puppy mills have thrived in Missouri since World War II. Fortunately the number of licensed puppy mills has gone down over the last ten years. Significantly tighter regulations and enforcement forced many closures. Others shut down due to the shaky economy and public education. In addition, many puppy mill owners were elderly and ready to retire.

In the early eighties, I began protesting in front of pet stores that sold these puppies. People at that time were unaware of what was going on with puppy mills, and many folks probably thought I was crazy. I loved going into mall pet stores and dropping stink bombs on the floor. They were little glass vials of some horrible liquid smelling of rotten eggs. I'd buy them from the local joke shop. They were made in Germany, and they came in little cardboard containers that said "Stinkbomen." I'd casually walk in the store (usually Petland or Pass Pets), drop the vial on the floor and step on it. Then I'd simply walk out of the store and take a comfortable seat in the aisle of the mall. I'd wait about one minute. Pretending I was a movie director, I loved knowing just when to say "action!" The customers would hurriedly rush out of the store holding their noses. It was perfect! Nobody gets hurt. The puppies don't smell anything because they are in a separate room behind glass. Nobody would dare step in the store for hours because people, it really stank. I did this off and on at different malls for years. In fact, just the other day I was cleaning out a storage cabinet and guess what I found? A whole box of unused Stinkbomen! Hmm.

By the year 2000, my anger and frustration increased to where I felt I needed to do more than just stand in front of malls with my friends and hold up protest signs. I had been to countless meetings where depressed animal lovers discussed the dog breeding industry. We had pamphlets and flyers and books and articles for everyone to look at. We knew all the statistics. I just couldn't take one more meeting. Nothing was changing. Dogs continued to suffer at the mills.

I decided that the best way to bring attention to the evils of the puppy mills was to walk across Missouri. So I did. In December of 2000, my German Shepherd, Scout, and I walked from the Mid Rivers Mall in St. Charles to Kansas City, a distance of about 250 miles.

A wonderful woman named Shirley Sostman helped me tremendously in organizing the walk. I knew nothing about press releases, but Shirley did. She also had contacts all across Missouri. She made sure there were people along the walk who could help me. She did a superb job, and I'll never forget her or how much she helped.

I decided to walk in December because the weather would be nice and cool. More importantly, I wanted to try and put a significant "dent" in Christmas puppy sales.

The big day came when Scout and I would begin our walk. Weather was perfect – in the 40s and 50s, and the sun was shining.

The media showed up. There were perhaps 30 or 40 people gathered around holding signs for the cameras. I was really happy my dad could make it too.

I was so proud of Scout. He looked awesome. He was an unusually large German Shepherd weighing 115 pounds. He was wearing a red and green backpack that held his food and my wallet, map, telephone and camera.

The "send off" ceremony lasted about an hour, and then it was time to go. My good friend Tim Monson walked with me for a few hours. I was so excited! I couldn't believe I was going to walk all the way to Kansas City. Scout and I were certainly on our way to adventure. Because of the media coverage around St. Louis, I was thrilled to receive a dozen or so horn honks and thumbs up from passersby. People would also stop their cars and run up to me with cash and chocolate brownies. The first day came and went quickly.

By nightfall, Scout was good and tired, and so was I. We checked into a motel and crashed. One day down, 15 more to go. As soon as we took off in the morning, I was astonished to watch Scout walk up to one parked car after another, where he would stand at the car's door and look at me as if to say, "Here's a perfectly good car. Let's drive this one." We followed the service road that ran parallel to the Interstate. We continued to walk, and by afternoon had waved to 20 or so horn –honking well-wishers.

My mother was very worried that the puppy mill people would try to kill me sometime during the walk. She kept saying in her thick Brooklyn accent, "Those puppy mill people are going to kill you, Gary! For God's sake, be careful!" "OK mom, "I'd reply. "Don't be silly." Or I'd say, "Don't be so dramatic. They might be assholes, but they aren't stupid." I really believed that. Unfortunately, I was wrong, and as usual, mom was right.

The morning of the third day as we were walking along a pretty secluded stretch of road, I noticed a white four-door sedan following us. They followed us from a distance of about 150 feet. They drove slowly, maybe one to two miles an hour. The surveillance lasted for a long five minutes. Finally they pulled up right behind me and they all got out of their car. There were two men in camouflage and coveralls wearing ball caps. The passenger in the front seat was an elderly man. The driver, a woman in her 60s, also got out of the car and said, "If you're so God damn worried about puppies, what are you doing forcing that "dawg" of yours to walk for hundreds of miles?"

I didn't say a word. The fat dude in the camouflage decided to "warn" me. "You bettah watch your tree-huggin' ass out here. You got a lot of enemies. You've been warned." With that, they put their car in reverse, backed into a cornfield a few feet, straightened the wheel and took off.

Nice. It took me a half hour or so to settle down after that little encounter. The weather was pleasant for December. The scenery was great. I noticed that the horn honking from supportive people began to fade as we were now probably 30 miles or so away from St. Louis.

The service road occasionally winds around and away from Interstate 70. Sometimes Scout and I would stop so I could take off our packs and rest for a bit. We'd eat a snack, maybe call home or touch base with Shirley. There were no smart phone back then, so I had few distractions. We'd walk a few miles, rest, walk a few more. Some days we'd walk 12 miles. Others 14 or 15. On the afternoon of the fifth day, a pickup truck pulled up right next to us and the guy motioned for me over to the cab of his truck. When I got about two feet from his window, he spit at me. He missed my face, but a little spray got me. He laughed and floored it. At this point I wished I had brought a handgun, just in case. But I was unarmed. We just kept walking. A couple of times people would pull up and say, "I saw you on T.V. I believe in what you are doing. Can I walk with you for a while? One nice woman walked with me for six or seven miles. I played my harmonica and sang. We shared stories. It made the miles go by faster.

Once in a while, local "rescue people" would bring Scout and me refreshments and some much needed conversation. Some nights we would sleep at the homes of some of Shirley's animal friends. One guy was a veterinarian who ran the local animal shelter.

About the sixth day of our journey, I began feeling some blisters on my feet. Shirley contacted some people who brought me some gel inserts for my shoes and some bandages for the blisters.

You have a lot of time to think about things when you are walking long distances. Sometimes people would look at me like I was a hobo or some kind of aging hippie vagabond. You also can get pretty damn hungry. One afternoon I ran out of water. "No biggie," I thought. I'll just go up to someone's house, explain what we're doing, and ask if I can fill my canteen. The first two or three houses pretty much just said, "No," and closed the door on us.

I was starving one day and amazingly, a friend of mine pulled up in his truck in the middle of nowhere and brought me some deer jerky. He had driven all the way from St. Louis County following the service road just to say hi and bring us the jerky. He took off after a few minutes, and Scout and I devoured the highly salted meat. Big mistake! I was out of water again and was beyond thirsty.

The days were getting noticeably colder now. Then the winds came. On the flat farmlands outside of Columbia, the wind really began to blow. It got cold, ice cold. There was no place to get out of the wind. We were about eight miles out of Columbia when we were lucky enough to find a feed store to get in out of the cold and the wind.

I began to wish that I had not made the trip so public. I wanted to give up, but I couldn't. All Scout and I could do was keep walking. A car stopped an hour or so later. They were women who had been contacted by Shirley. They all volunteered at a local animal shelter and were super nice. They brought us some snacks and told us they would be waiting for us at the Columbia exit five miles or so ahead. Best of all, they took my back pack as well as Scout's just to lighten our load. What a treat. To my delight, they gave Scout a fleece jacket to keep him warm. He wore that jacket throughout the rest of the walk, and as it turned out, he needed it. Nearly every day for the rest of our walk, we did interviews at radio stations. We also did a 10 or 15 minute TV studio interview that went really well. The TV hosts were really anti puppy mill and asked many intelligent questions. I was ecstatic. After all, this was the whole point of the walk.

The day of the big TV interview, the weather turned extremely cold, and was snowing like hell. I was in the middle of a complete white out. Walking along with Scout, the countryside looked like Antarctica. I'm not going to lie to you. I was pretty scared. Whenever I thought about calling it all off, I thought about how bad the dogs in the Missouri puppy mills had it. Trust me, folks. I'm no martyr, but I do love dogs deeply. So we just kept walking, mile after mile. The weather deteriorated even more. Typical of my luck, this December turned out to be one of the coldest in Missouri's history. On one of the last days of the walk, Scout and I were supposed be staying with some animal friends overnight. The weather was so bad that they couldn't drive to us in the blizzard-like conditions. We found an old motel to crash in that was, uh, well, interesting to say the least. The room reeked of mildew and cigarettes. The lumpy bed took up almost the entire room, and the TV had one working station – the Disney Channel. The shower was full of dead roaches, and I spotted mouse droppings on the bathroom floor.

I tried to get a room at a newer, nicer place down the road, but that one didn't allow dogs. Outside of my motel room, perhaps 100 yards away, was an adult book store. Interestingly, there was a well-worm path (visible even in the storm) that went from the room to the book store.

It stopped snowing overnight, and the sun was shining, but the temperature continued to plummet. I was dressed for it. Long johns, wool socks, insulated boots, down coat, and insulated pants and gloves, but I worried about my best friend, Scout. The coat the women brought him really helped. He never seemed to mind the cold at all, and we suffered no frost bite.

It just so happened that on the very coldest and snowiest day of the trek, Scout and I walked almost 16 miles. Shirley had arranged for us to spend the night at the Super 8 motel in New Florence. I was so tired when I saw the motel from a distance, I almost cried with joy. By the time we reached the parking lot at the motel, I could hardly speak. I was shocked to see that the staff at the motel had erected a large banner above the lobby that that said, "Welcome Honored Guests. Gary and Scout." They had also plastered newspaper articles about us from all over the state in the front window of the lobby. When we walked in the lobby, we saw a couple of dozen people waiting for us. They broke into applause, and I just started crying with surprise, happiness, and relief. The mayor, the police chief, and even the local Catholic priest were there to say hello and welcome. There was a large Christmas tree, and they had placed a table in the center of the lobby for me to sit and eat a wonderful Christmas dinner. And there's more. A certified animal massage therapist was on hand to massage Scout. I was so overwhelmed by all of the kindness shown to Scout and me. The staff at the motel had made a little Christmas ornament that I still hang on my Christmas tree to this day. On one side it says, "Puppy Mill Awareness." On the other side, "Gary Abelov and Scout. Honored Guests." After all the food and cheer, they took my soaked clothes and Scout's jacket and laundered them for us. Scout and I retired to our warm bed and were fast asleep within seconds.

The trip ended at a large shopping mall in Kansas City where there was a Petland store. Several well-wishers and protestors carrying anti puppy mill signs were there to meet me. The media had been alerted, and a camera crew from Kansas City television was on hand. I walked into the Petland store and handed the young lady behind the counter a pamphlet that talked about Missouri's puppy mills. I smiled at her and said, "I walked all the way across Missouri just to hand this to you." As I turned to leave the store, three male security cops said, "Sir, you will have to leave the mall immediately." I didn't mind. I had no shopping to do. Besides, the camera caught it all which made me very very happy.

My friends waiting for me in the mall parking lot helped load my pack into their SUV for the trip home.

I will never forget the look on Scout's face. He was so happy when I said, "It's ok buddy. Hop in. It's time to go home!"

A few minutes later we were on the Interstate. I watched Scout looking out the window of the car. He turned his head to look at me, lay down, and let out a big sigh.

On the Walk Across Missouri

Gary Abelov
and Scout will

WALK ACROSS MISSOURI

THE # 1 PUPPY MILL STATE

TO BRING ATTENTION TO THE "MILLS" AND PET STORE PUPPIES

starting on monday
December 4 at 10:30 am
Mid Rivers Mall
St. Peters

Gary and Scout join the protest.

Taking a break at the feed store in Missouri.

At the Kansas City Petland.

Asked to leave the mall.

Ryan Prewitt photo

Gary Abelov, with Scout, is planning to walk to Kansas City to raise awareness about the cruel treatment of canines in puppy mills across the state.

Taking a break.

Gary Abelov

Classes

People often ask if I teach group classes. My answer: No. I'm not opposed to group classes. Learning with your dog in a class setting can be a fun and rewarding experience if you have a great teacher.

I work with the dogs that have been expelled from school for one reason or another. The fighters, biters, chronic barkers, hyperactive and seriously fearful dogs usually either flunk out or are politely asked to not come back.

I make house calls. Lots and lots of them, about four hundred or so a year. I choose to see dogs with behavioral problems in their homes, privately, one on one, with their people watching and often joining in. While there may be distractions in the dog's home while I'm there, those distractions are nothing compared to what takes place in a public building. By making house calls, I can see for myself how a dog acts in his yard and at his front door. Most importantly, a dog will be as relaxed as he possibly can be in his own familiar environment. At the dog's home, I can check out crates, dog doors, windows, yard, and the layout of the home's interior.

It's not that I wouldn't enjoy the luxury of having people come to me with their dogs. I could save all of the wear and tear on both myself and my car. I wouldn't have to eat out as often as I do. With all the money I'd save on gas each day, I could order in! Also, I could make quite a bit more money. Wouldn't that be nice? Sure, no traveling all over the city and county. I could see more dogs. Best of all there would never be any interruptions! No phone calls. No lawn people, landlords, repair men and kids crying and hassling mom. Yes sir, it would be sweet.

It just won't work, though. I have to see them at home if I'm really going to help them. Believe me, I've wracked my brains trying to figure out another way, but it's no use. Besides, look at all the fun and adventure I've been having all of these years while visiting people's homes.

Some of my clients have been to group classes in the past and were not pleased with their dogs' behavior or performance at the class's conclusion. If you are fortunate enough to live near a quality group training class and you have a well-behaved dog, by all means go!

A good class will have about 10 students with an experienced instructor who is certified with appropriate credentials. The instructor should demonstrate respect and kindness towards both the dogs and their guardians.

A quality instructor avoids choke, prong or shock collars. These are antiquated tools that can and often do cause more harm than good. Look for a trainer that proudly utilizes positive methods including lots of praise and love, clickers and food rewards. Ask for references and check them! Never assume that trainers "know their stuff" just because they say they do. Check 'em out before you sign on the line! It's critically important to work with a solid, caring, experienced professional. That goes double if you have a fearful or aggressive dog.

Group classes have a very high dropout rate. Surprisingly, this happens even when you have a good, quality instructor. It's not the instructor's fault. People sign up with enthusiasm initially, but life gets in the way. Vacations, sick kids, overtime at work, relationship problems all contribute to this high rate of attrition.

I've seen many people drop out of group classes because their dog is not progressing. Your Bulldog or Bloodhound may not learn as quickly as the Border Collie to your right or the German Shepherd to your left. As a result, people blame the trainer or think their dog is "stupid." All dogs learn at different rates, a fact may instructors fail to mention. Everyone is expected to teach their dogs at the same pace over what is usually a six-week course. It just doesn't work that way for many people and their dogs, so they drop out, and often dogs that could have learned enough to help them stay in their homes, end up in shelters or are "put to sleep."

I estimate that at least three of every 10 people who enroll in a group training class will quit. Recently I helped a young couple with their Great Dane. They had recently graduated from a novice obedience class. In their class, of the thirteen dogs that started, theirs was the only one who completed the course.

As I mentioned earlier, a group class is traditionally an hour in duration. Six classes is the norm. You and your furry kid are to show up once a week at a predetermined time. You are expected to work with your dog at home between classes. All dogs are expected to progress at the same rate. I think this "get 'em in, get 'em out", assembly line approach to training is without intelligence and imagination and is really detrimental to a quality education.

If you have a dog that learns more slowly than other breeds, make sure to discuss this with your instructor before you sign up. Not sure about your dog's level of working intelligence? All breeds have been thoroughly tested and evaluated and ranked according to their learning ability. A simple google search will enable you to find that information. Ask your trainer if remedial sessions are available at no additional charge if you and your dog are struggling. Will they be free or offered to you at a discounted rate?

Remember: Never join any class, private or public, before

- Checking the trainer's or behavior consultant's credentials
- Asking how many years of experience the trainer has.
- Asking for and checking references
- Finding out about methodology and use of equipment
- Asking about the policy concerning dogs that learn more slowly

For the most part, I advise staying away from pet store dog training classes. Yes, they are conveniently located and are pretty inexpensive. My clients complain to me about them regularly. As a rule, this is where trainers start their careers. Don't let them learn on your dog.

Pet stores don't care about excellence in training. They basically want to get you into their store each week for six weeks. In some corporate board room, they have discussed and analyzed how much money the average person will end up spending in their store while enrolled in their class.

Let's just say your class is just $100. Each week you will pass by leashes and treats, dog crates and toys, nail clippers and, well, you get the picture. By the completion of the class, you might have spent several hundred or even a thousand dollars on your dog. Spread over six weeks, lots of folks will not even notice. Oh, don't forget to buy her more toys and a new rawhide while you're there.

Good quality dog trainers usually don't stay at pet stores for too long. I've personally known five or six wonderful trainers who left pet stores for greener pastures. They were pressured by management to constantly push students to buy merchandise and sign people up for more classes, even when they didn't need or want them.

The next time you walk into a big chain pet store, chances are pretty good you'll see a sign as you walk in that says, "P/T Pet Trainer wanted."

Classes can be an excellent and inexpensive learning experience for you and your dog. If you do a little research and pick your trainer/school wisely, most dog guardians should be happy with the results.

But if your dog has behavioral issues, group classes are not the place to try to resolve them. If you need help finding a good class, private trainer or behavior specialist, check the following websites. They have state by state lists of experienced, qualified people to help you.

Association of Professional Dog Trainers
information@apdt.com

International Association of Animal Behavior Consultants
information@iaabc.org

Typical List Handed to Me at a Consultation

- Pulled out of collar last Tuesday
- Pulled out of collar and jumped the fence last Wednesday
- Tried to pull out of walking harness last Thursday during walk
- Goes over end tables instead of jumping on floor and walking around.
- Pogo jumps and grabs clothing while in air
- Protective of unopened food bags and shows teeth when Toffee gets too close
- Was wild in car and fought with Sadie
- Barks at and wants to chase birds
- Barks inside while crated and when I'm outside working
- Keeps trying to jump on lap even while I'm at table eating
- Jumps on table and eats cat's food.
- Chases the cats just for the heck of it
- House soiling
- Desk Chewer
- Very timid when meeting someone new
- Leash chewer

Secret in Suburbia

Their Golden Retriever performed beautifully. Lisa and Paul looked on as I completed our last of five basic obedience lessons. I asked their dog to sit and stay for several minutes and ran him through a number of other commands. Then with the Golden sitting about 50 feet from me, I called him to me. He ran up to me enthusiastically and sat right in front of me as he had done so many times before.

I happily handed the couple their dog's graduation certificate, shook their hands and told them how proud I was of their effort and accomplishment.

During the weeks I'd visited Lisa and Paul's home, I'd noticed three or four people, all adults, coming and going. They never knocked or rang the doorbell. They just came into the house through the garage and into the kitchen. They usually stopped long enough to say hello before going down into the basement. They seemed very friendly, so I assumed Paul and Lisa ran a business out of their home. One day I learned just what kind of business they were operating. It happened after Lisa offered me a glass of wine. It was the end of my work day, so I said yes. I followed Paul and Lisa through the sliding glass door to a beautifully landscaped yard with a pool. The pool had a slide and a fountain. Ah, the good life, I thought, as we relaxed and began talking.

A lively conversation followed, loosened perhaps by the wine. We discussed politics, religion, restaurants, and cars, among other things. We shared similar opinions about most things.

I told Paul that I had loved Volkswagens all my life. He was surprised and said most of the guys he knew preferred "muscle" cars. I explained that in Southern California, where I grew up during the "swinging sixties," VWs were part of the culture. I was a surfer and for a time thought of myself as a hippie. "In fact, my girlfriend and our dogs traveled all over the country in our VW camper," I volunteered. Lisa and Paul, though not a part of that era, were interested in the music.

Had I been to Woodstock? No, but wished I'd been there. Had I been to any concerts? Oh yeah. Hendrix, The Doors. The Stones. No, I'd never seen the Beatles, but I once sat on a piano bench with Janis Joplin when she performed at the Pavilion in Forest Park

The conversation turned to the topic of living off the grid in the country. We also discussed solar and wind power and agreed that we'd all "go green" if we ever built another house. Lisa then asked if I wanted to smoke a little weed. My first reaction was "no." I'd left all that behind long ago." Lisa asked again. "It's pretty mellow stuff." Maybe that last line was what changed my mind. Or maybe it was my relaxed state next to the pool. So "Hell, why not." I said.

I have to admit the grass smelled and tasted pretty good. After a couple of tokes, I knew that I had better stop. Better safe than sorry. After all, it had been decades since I'd last smoked. Better tread lightly.

"So, Paul," I asked. "What do you do for a living, may I ask?"

"We are in the nursery business," he answered.

"Oh really? Do you have a nursery or …" I wasn't sure what I was asking.

Paul stood and said, "C'mon. I'll show you." Soon I was following both of them back through the house and down into the basement. At the bottom of the steps, I noticed a fireplace with a flat screen television hanging over it, a pool table, small bar, and to my surprise a slot machine. "Does it work?" "Yeah, sure. Give it a try." I did. I put my nickel in the slot, pulled the lever, and got one cherry and two peaches. I lost. Oh well.

"Are you ready, Gary?" asked Paul, and he opened a door on the far side of the room. What I saw next completely caught me off guard. Apparently, my clients were in the marijuana business. Wow! Yesseree Bob! Arranged in neat rows were several hundred or so pot plants.   Each plant was in a large pot. Grow lights ran the full length of the room in four strips. White PVC pipes irrigated the plants. Lisa showed me the air filtration system and explained to me how they kept the utility company from noticing the large amount of electricity they consumed daily. "We have solar panels on the far side of the house that nobody can really see. It cuts our electricity bill in half."

I was pretty shocked. I had seen people grow a plant or two back in the early seventies, but I had never, ever seen anything of this magnitude. It wasn't what one would expect in this upscale neighborhood in conservative St. Louis County.

What really amazed me was that these people trusted me enough to reveal all of this to me.

I had to ask. "Why do you show me this?"

"We just trust you Gary," they both said.

I was pretty flattered.

Gary Abelov

Bartering

On occasion clients will call me and offer to barter for my services. They are short on cash and I'm afraid that if we can't figure out some form of payment, they will turn their dog into a shelter. Instead of denying them my help, I will ask what they have to offer in trade. Following is a list of the things I've taken in exchange for dog training.

- Tarot Card Reading
- Haircuts
- Massages
- Guitar lessons
- Chocolate brownies
- House cleaning
- Chimney cleaning
- Bottles of Wine
- Dance lessons
- Copper mailbox
- Birdhouse (hand-made)
- Antique typewriter
- Auto upholstery repair
- Driveway sealcoating
- Dog grooming
- Blacksmith tools
- Business cards
- Pen and Ink house portrait
- Handmade deer antler knife
- Framed art
- Large antique lard can
- Silver and Turquoise belt buckle
- '60s psychedelic concert poster
- Carpet cleaning
- Hibachi
- Firewood

- Antique ice cream cooler
- Porcelain dog figurines
- Auto detailing
- Chicken and duck eggs
- Garden vegetables
- Men and Dogs

I'm always slightly surprised when my phone rings and it's a male caller. They do call occasionally but in disproportionately low numbers compared to women. Of my last 100 home consultations, only 20 originated with male callers.

As a man, I get a little twitchy when I hear women making negative comments about men, such as "Men never talk." Or "Guys will never ask for help or for directions." I have been asking for directions from locals and gas stations for more than 40 years. I've gotten lost everywhere from the East Village in New York City to the Mayan ruins in Mexico and almost every place in between. I've used this useful Spanish sentence a hundred times or more. "Dónde está la playa? (Where is the beach?)"

I'm actually very good at getting hopelessly lost, and I've never hesitated to ask for directions. I've also been a responsible and loving single father, so I bristle a little when I hear people talking about dead- beat dads.

I've defended my gender many times, so it upsets me that my fellow men so often let me down by doing stupid things, such as not showing up at the consultation their wife or girlfriend set up. If the session is on a Saturday, the men are more likely to be there initially but will often leave about 30 minutes after the session begins with a quick look at their watch and an apologetic, "Gary, I am so sorry. It's been great listening to you, but I have to go." Sometimes he will also look at his wife and say, "Don't I, honey?" He'll usually stand up, shake my hand and vanish, as they say, "in two shakes of a dog's tail."

Here are the top 10 excuses men give for vanishing from a dog training session.

- Have to pick up the kids
- Have an important appointment
- Going to a sporting event
- Have to pick up a friend
- Have to pick up a friend because we're going fishing/hunting, etc.
- Expecting an important call
- Don't feel well/sick
- Have to go into work
- Need to help a friend with an urgent problem
- Have a doctor's appointment I forgot about

It's absolutely predictable. I'm actually shocked when a guy makes it all the way through the session. Suburban guys are the worst. Young men (20s to mid-30s) nearly always stay to the end. City guys stay longer. Affluent men? They never sit through the entire consultation.

So what does it mean? Beats me.

Men loves dogs as much as women do. Some are very interested in their dog's training and general care. However, when it comes to receiving instruction on dog training from someone like me, men are more often than not MIA.

Gary Abelov

Mr. Shaggs

The first time I laid eyes on Shaggs, I was struck by how beautiful a dog he was. He was as handsome an Old English Sheepdog as I had ever seen.

Shagg's people called me because he had eaten five pounds of freshly made fudge off of the kitchen counter. The fudge was intended for my clients' Church Parish picnic to be held on the following day. Poor Mr. Shaggs barfed over and over all night long. Shaggs's mom said she held his head in her lap and stroked him all night until the sun came up. Finally, Shaggs fell soundly asleep and my client slipped into the bathroom to take a shower. After hurriedly getting dressed, she returned to the sunroom to check on her sick dog.

Shaggs wasn't sleeping. He wasn't in the sunroom. Oh no! Shaggs was in the kitchen finishing off an entire apple pie, tin and all.

Mr. Shaggs, you are truly a piece of work.

Gary Abelov

Top 10 Mistakes Newbie Dog Guardians Make

- Purchasing dog from pet store, puppy mill or an amateur "hobby" breeder. Instead, adopt a dog from a local shelter or rescue group. If you simply must have a purebred puppy, do some serious research and find a reputable breeder with sterling references.

- Selecting an inappropriate breed for the family and/or resident dog. Think. Will your 12-year-old Bichon appreciate your bringing home a rambunctious Golden Retriever?

- Failing to give the dog enough exercise daily.

- Failing to spay or neuter the dog

- Deciding not to train their dog

- Being overly permissive

- Failing to socialize the dog with children, strangers and other dogs

- Hoping the dog will simply outgrow its destructive, obnoxious and/or aggressive behavior.

- Wrongly adhering to a popular but archaic idea that dogs only learn when you "catch them in the act" and then punish them. Instead of trying to catch them doing awful things, try instead to catch them doing good things and reward them for it using praise, clickers, and treats. Positive reinforcement is your best option.

- Giving young, immature and untrained dogs too much physical freedom too soon

Pup Needs Training

BEST FRIENDS Dog Training Systems, Obedience, Problem Dogs, Counseling. Call Gary 256-0860

My First Ad.

It certainly seemed like an easy job. A woman called me and asked if I could come over and answer some questions she had concerning her three-month-old puppy.

"I need some help with the potty thing. Also, I need help teaching him how to walk on a leash."

Oh, and there was one other thing. She thought it would be a good idea if her kids could sit in on the consultation. After all, she said, "They begged me to get the puppy and promised to help take care of it."

The house was in an historic neighborhood where turn-of-the-century street lamps lined the sidewalks. Everything spoke of wealth and comfort, from the Spanish style clay tile roof to the enormous rounded oak front door, complete with hand-forged hinges.

A strikingly beautiful woman in her mid- thirties answered the door and greeted me warmly.

"Hi Gary. Hey kids, Mr. Abelov the dog trainer is here!" Mom (I'll call her Christine) escorted me into their living room. I sat down on a hard- back chair in front of an antique wooden table. Christine introduced me to Pip, her new puppy, a terribly cute Border Collie mix.

Suddenly, Christine turned from me to yell at her still absent children.

"Let's go. C'mon. We're waiting!"

We talked for a couple of minutes as I picked up Pip and pet him a few times as he licked my face. Mom's mood darkened again. "Emily! Josh! Come in here right now!"

71

Finally, they appeared. A boy about 12, toting a white laptop computer, stomped in and slumped into another chair by the table, immediately opening his laptop. Josh's younger sister, Emily, seemed just as annoyed as her brother as she took her place at the table.

I started the consultation by asking the kids how they liked their new puppy. They stared at me but said nothing. Josh folded his arms defiantly across his chest. Tension built as Christine reached across the table and slammed her son's computer shut.

"I want you to pay attention!' she barked.

I smiled and soldiered on, talking about how to housebreak a new puppy. I would have preferred a friendly environment, but I figured I could work past the tension. I thought it was weird, but I didn't know then just how weird it would soon become.

I had just begin talking when Christine's husband arrived home in his silver Porsche. He greeted Christine with a "Hi, baby," introduced himself to me as Craig, and then turned to the children, asking if they really wanted to be there. "No!" they shouted, and dad said they could leave. I expected the worst, especially when Christine's eyes narrowed to slits and she asked her husband to follow her into the kitchen so she could "speak to him." They closed the kitchen door behind them but I could hear just enough to know she was giving him a piece of her mind for undermining her authority. I wondered if I should just sneak out the door.

I hate when couples fight. Especially when I'm trying to conduct a consultation. It doesn't happen that often, but more often than I would like. One variation of couple fighting really vexes me. That's when dogs are squabbling with each other, and the guardians are taking sides. One person will be sitting on one side of the room with one dog and the other on the opposite side with the other dog. The woman will say it's all "his" dogs fault. He says, "Her dog is the one that starts all the trouble." I always try to remind the couple that there can't be a "my dog" vs "your dog." They are both "your dogs."

While I'm having these thoughts, Christine and Craig emerged from the kitchen, and the tension between the two of them was palpable. What happened next can only be described as, well, awkward. Christine took the seat to my left. She scooted forward towards the edge of her seat, making room as Craig swung a leg over the chair and squeezed in behind her. OK. Kind of weird. But ok.

So I continued on about rewarding Pip outside after she eliminated. I emphasized the importance of praise and how punishment has no place in housetraining dogs.

All at once, Craig placed his hands on his wife's shoulders and started massaging them. He stopped the shoulder massage after a few seconds and began rubbing the sides of her neck. Christine occasionally closed her eyes and leaned her head back just slightly. I've probably taught a thousand people how to potty train a dog, but this was the very first time I'd taught someone while they were receiving (and giving) a sensual massage. But I boldly talked on. When Christine started making little circles with head, Craig moved his hands up and down her back. Up and down. Up and down.

They continued and so did I, explaining that they should keep a journal of Pip's elimination habits for one week. "Write down every time you take her out. Make a note whether she eliminates or not. If you feed and water at the same time each day, a very clear cut elimination pattern will emerge. This will help you recognize your puppy's body posture when he needs to go. You won't need to waste a lot of time waiting outside for Pip to go to the bathroom."

Although the massage continued, Christine and Craig did seem to be listening. So I talked on, but then Craig dropped his chin onto Christine's shoulder and began massaging the outside of her thighs. OK. Enough, I thought. Enough. I decided to take some action of my own. I suggested we take Pip outside so I could show them how to get him to walk nicely on a leash. I hated to interrupt their little petting session (not really), but I was afraid of what might happen next.

The remainder of the training session was fairly normal. We took turns walking the puppy for maybe 20 minutes, and both Christine and Craig seemed very relaxed. I, on the other hand, was now quite tense. But our session was almost over.

When we walked back to the house, Craig wrote me a check and I left. Later that day, I looked at the check and saw that Craig had given me a $150 tip. I wasn't sure what to think. Were they swingers? Exhibitionists? Or just really weird people who give great tips. You tell me.

My favorite dog myths

- **Pitbulls have special locking jaws.** Not true. Powerful jaws, yes. Do they "lock" in some unusual way? No.

- **Dogs can smell fear.** Not so. They can, of course, smell all kinds of things that we would never notice. Can they tell you are afraid because you are sweating? The answer is no. They can, however, detect that you are afraid by observing your body language or become alarmed because you are staring at them. These things, and others, can certainly cause a dog to think you are acting strangely, and as a result they may be "on alert."

- **German Shepherds will suddenly "turn on you."** This is a good one. I've heard this all my life. Interestingly, I've never had a woman say this to me. Only senior citizen males. Since I haven't heard this recently, I'm hoping this particular myth is on the way out.

- **Feeding expensive dog food will increase your dog's longevity.** I admit that I pay big money for my dogs' food. I purchase food that is corn and grain free. The chicken is antibiotic and hormone free. I like that the food has omega 3 fatty acids and fish meal. Why do I spend the extra money? Because I love them, and it makes me feel better to give them the best. However, there is no scientific evidence that a specific diet of quality food will add years to a dog's life. But the debate rages on over which diet is best. Raw meat and fresh vegetables vs commercially prepared kibble. Grain free and hormone free. Chelated minerals vs regular. Some dog food companies project an image of wholesome ingredients only to have their expensive, premium dog food recalled, sometimes over and over. At the time of this writing, the largest pet food manufacturer in the world is suing a well-known "natural premium" food manufacturer for false advertising. For many years I fed my dogs "grocery store" brands and they lived healthy, long lives. Only time will tell if my current dog food choices will add years or energy to my dogs' lives. I have concluded that if your dog is thriving on the food you feed her, great. Stick with it. The jury is still out on the question of diet and its effect on the longevity of dogs.

- **Dogs with backyards are happier and healthier than those that live in apartments.** Having a fenced backyard can be a wonderful luxury. You simply let you dog out, and he can wander around and do whatever he pleases. I've noticed, however, that dogs are rarely self-motivated when it comes to exercise. Sure, puppies will run outside and frolic on their own. But as they mature, you'll notice that the romping around slows down. By the time most dogs are 18 months to two years, they simply go into the yard to do a bit of exploring and to relieve themselves. They'll look around to see if anything unusual has taken place in their absence. Then they'll walk back to the door and wait for you to let them back in. Some of the most poorly exercised, bored and lonely dogs I have ever seen have large backyards. Some of the happiest and most physically fit dogs I've met lived in high rise apartment building in the middle of the city. I know this sounds crazy, but it really is true. A dog in an apartment or condo has to be taken for several "potty walks" a day. They see the doorman, other tenants, other dogs, street vendors, musicians, and who knows what else.

- **Mutts are always healthier than purebreds and vice versa.** Proponents of either side like to use the word "always." That's where the problem is. Purebreds can be healthy or can have huge health issues, and so can mixed breed dogs.

- **Feeding garlic to your dog will prevent him from getting fleas.** There is no evidence that garlic will control fleas on dogs. If you suspect your dog has fleas, contact your veterinarian and ask about newer flea control products. Inexpensive they're not, but they are safe and highly effective. Many of my clients have turned to "natural" or "organic" flea control products for various reasons. I've always found the "natural" products to be ineffective and sometimes unsafe. Further, garlic given in large doses to dogs can be toxic.

- **Dogs eat their own feces (coprophagia) because of a nutritional imbalance.** Not true, according to a scientific study conducted in the late '80s. Coprophagic dogs were separated into several groups. One group received multi vitamins, one group received a high quality kibble, another group received a standard "grocery store" dog food, and the remaining group received additional fiber. The study saw no change in the dogs' poop-eating habits. Dogs in all groups continued to eat their poop. It seems that some dogs just like the taste of not only dog feces, but also cat, horse, rabbit and chicken poo. For many dogs, these things are delicacies.

- **When a dog has behavioral problems, it's almost always the fault of its guardian.** This widely held belief has actually increased in popularity over the past five to 10 years. However, I have seen thousands of dogs who through absolutely no fault of their guardians are, shall we say, behaviorally challenged. These problems can be genetically inherited or they may be learned through the dog's life experiences.

- **Little dogs are hard to potty train because they have little bladders.** I admit that I do see a disproportionately large number of small dogs with house soiling problems. However, it's not because of their tiny bladders. Yes, their bladders are small, but they are in correct proportion to their bodies. Small dogs drink the appropriate amount of water for their size and their bladders can handle it. So why do so many people have so much trouble housebreaking small dogs? Many small dog lovers overly humanize their dogs. I like to call this the "Paris Hilton" syndrome. They actually will carry their dogs everywhere. Instead, they should be teaching their dogs to walk to an appropriate elimination spot outside the house. It can also be more difficult to supervise little dogs as they can easily disappear behind a piece of furniture or slip into another room. Once they develop a preference for going in the house, it is hard to redirect them to the yard. People who adopt or purchase small dogs usually do so with the express purpose of babying them. They simply cannot bring themselves to crate train (feel crates are mean), or they can't bear to hear their dog cry while gated in the kitchen. We must also consider the intelligence factor. Certain breeds may take considerably longer to understand what is expected of them. As a result, when the housebreaking process takes longer than expected, people either start punishing their dog or simply give up and start placing "potty pads" on their floors.

- **A dog should never sleep in bed with you or be allowed on furniture because it will then think it's the "alpha."**

- **Dogs are great judges of a person's character. If a dog dislikes someone, there's something wrong with that individual.** No. Dogs do not possess supernatural abilities. They can smell things that we can't and in most cases can hear far better than humans. I find these abilities to be nothing short of amazing. Yet they can't look inside a human's eyes and detect character flaws. Dogs can become afraid of or be put off by people who cherish dogs and would never hurt a fly. All too often well-meaning people try too hard to win over a shy, timid or nervous dog. They move too quickly to gain a dog's trust. When they do, the dog and human become very much like repelling magnets. Let dogs take their time getting to know you. Trying to hurry the process will only cause the dog to become more reluctant to accept you.

- **Shelter dogs carry a lot of baggage, so it's better to buy a puppy and start off fresh.** Well maybe. But most shelter dogs I meet have few if any behavior problems. When they do, many rescue groups and shelters work with a behavior specialist to help the dog through its problems. Buying or adopting puppies is not without its problems. Pups can be chewing and pooping machines. Are you ready for the jumping, chewing and crazy energy of a young dog?

- **A dog cannot really be healthy and happy unless it can run off leash.**

- **Playing Tug of War causes aggression.**

- **Dogs only see in black and white.**

- **When dogs are ready to die, they "go off to the woods to die."** There isn't much to this old myth. The dog that "went off somewhere to die" in reality just got lost, was hit by a car, was stolen or was found by some kind person who has kept him.

- **A warm or dry nose means your dog is sick.**

- **The best way to teach a dog right from wrong is to "catch them in the act and then punish them.** This myth has been around for many decades. The best and most effective way to teach a dog is to limit its freedom when it is immature and curious. This will eliminate a great deal of chewing and digging. Patiently teaching them and molding their behavior using positive reinforcement is the way to go. As the dog matures, it can be rewarded with more and more freedom.

- **Female dogs should have a litter puppies before they are spayed.**

- **Male dogs should experience sex at least once before they are neutered.**

- **Dogs age seven years for every human year.** Multiplying by seven is how most people calculate their dog's age. Unfortunately, the method is highly inaccurate. Dogs mature and grow quickly compared to humans. They can grow from birth to puberty in one to two years. After that, the aging process slows down considerably. Try this instead. Subtract two from your dog's age. Then multiply that by four and add 21. That would make a five year old dog equivalent to a 33 year old, a 10-year old equivalent to a 53 year old. Remember also that small dogs generally live longer than large and giant breeds.

- **You can't teach an old dog new tricks.**

- **A dog's mouth is cleaner than a human's.**

- **Dogs destroy your personal items (shoes, clothing, and furniture) because they are angry at you.** Dogs chew to relieve pressure and tension and because it's pleasurable to do. More often than not, destructive chewers are younger dogs (ages four months to 18 months). Frequently they receive too little exercise and mental stimulation and too much freedom too soon.

- **Dogs feel guilt just like people do.** No. Guilt and shame are human emotions. Behaviorists say dogs experience no guilt even though their folks say otherwise. That look of "shame and remorse" on a dog's face (ears lowered, head lowered, tail tucked) is likely due to scolding, gasping, spanking and pointing. The guilty look on a dog's face is a submissive response to a stressful encounter or situation. It means "please don't hurt me. Please don't be angry. I'm sorry, etc. "

- **If you don't dominate your dog, he will try to dominate you.** This popular myth is based on the erroneous assumption that wolves fight amongst themselves for "alpha status." This is untrue for wolves and for domestic dogs.

- **Once a dog has gotten a taste of blood, it will always want to kill.**

Gary Abelov

The Cave

Every day I look forward to meeting new dogs of every description. Big and small, fat and skinny, timid and pushy. I also love seeing their homes.

Most of the dogs I see live in typical suburban subdivisions. The newer subdivisions often have street names that have little to do with their surroundings. For example, Wild Cherry Parkway contains no cherry trees. Merlo Lane and Chardonnay Avenue are nowhere near any vineyards or wineries. Many of the older subdivision have streets named after the developer's family members.   So Paula Avenue runs into Mary Anne Drive which runs into Norma Street. And as I noted before, in North St. Louis County many of the streets bear the names of saints.

I'll admit it. I grow tired of subdivisions where all the homes look alike. I'm delighted when a consultation takes me somewhere out of the ordinary. As a dog trainer, I've been to high rise condos and apartments, retail stores, swank penthouses, four family flats and even tenements. I've taught dogs to sit in trailers, houseboats, and on many farms and horse ranches. I once trained a dog in a boarding stable. I also visited a dog in a homemade Geodesic Dome, and once I trained a dog who lived in a fabulous tree house. The tree house dog's guardian was a saddle maker. Seriously!

I thought I'd seen pretty much every kind of dwelling out there until the day I pulled up in front of a cave. I rechecked my directions. Yes. This was it. Five family members and a 12-week old German Shepherd pup lived together in a huge cave in Crystal City. And what a cave it was! My jaw dropped as a sat in my car stunned. The entire front of this massive cave was made of recycled sliding glass doors. After I met my new clients, they told me that me that the temperature inside the cave never changed, even in Missouri's volatile weather. It remained at 62 degrees year around.

learned that the cave was originally a limestone mine. When
limestone vein dried up, the cave became a sandstone mine for a
neighboring glass factory. Years later the cave was converted into a
roller skating rink named Caveland. Best of all, Caveland held
numerous concerts that featured the likes of Ike and Tina Turner,
Ted Nugent, Bob Seeger, Mc5 and even Chuck Berry.

Today, the 15,000 square foot cave was the home to a wonderful
family. Mom, dad and three children. The youngest was born at
home…yes…in the cave. Within the walls of Caveland, Dad had
built a modern three story, three bedroom home with every possible
convenience. Also within the walls of the cave was a hydroponic
Tilapia farm.

Next to the family's residence was the former stadium which
was the size of a football field. When the family showed me the
stadium, I lost control. I couldn't help myself. I hopped up on the
stage and looked around, singing a few licks of Bob Seeger lyrics
and even a bit from Chuck Berry. It was hard to remember why I
was there since I was having too much fun. But soon enough we
settled down to working with the puppy and his typical puppy
problems.

As I left, I thought, "Nobody will ever believe this," but yet,
there it was: Caveland!

Hollywood

Phone calls that come early in the morning or late at night make me twitch and jump. More often than not, these calls bring bad news.

For a number of years my parents were sick and frail and sometimes fell down and hurt themselves. I worried about them all of the time, and I often got calls from someone informing me that they were in the emergency room.

Then there's my son the cop. Jarret likes to chase down bad guys and tackle them. He's called me several times from the hospital after he's been injured.

Things have calmed down in the last few years. My folks have both passed away. Jarret still gets hurt while on duty, but there are fewer E.R. visits. So now if the phone rings at odd times, I don't get too excited. I figure it's probably a salesperson.

One morning last fall I heard the phone ring while I was busy feeding my dogs. I glanced at the clock on the kitchen counter. It said 8 a.m. I didn't recognize the phone number. Caller ID just said "New York City." I thought, "Should I answer it?" I almost didn't. But thinking it might be a potential client, I changed my mind and picked up. The caller identified himself as Todd Miller, the Casting Director at Animal Planet. "Do you have a minute?" he asked.

"Well sure," I said, and soon learned that Miller produced a television show on Animal Planet called "My Cat from Hell" and that he was now creating a new show and wondered if I'd like to be involved. "Involved?" I replied. With the phone at my ear, I finished feeding my dogs while also realizing that I hadn't had my first cup of coffee yet. "What's your show going to be about and how can I help?" I asked while searching my cupboard for coffee filters.

Todd replied, "The name of the show is 'My Tiny Terror.' Would you like to be a part of this project?"

"Are you looking for a technical adviser?" I asked.

"Well, no. The show will be about out-of-control little dogs. Each episode will feature a trainer who makes house calls and helps the dog's behavior improve."

"You mean a different trainer every week?" I asked.

"No," Todd said. "If we select you, the show would revolve around you."

I started to laugh out loud "Is this some kind of joke?"

"Oh no, Gary. I can assure you this is not a joke. We are pitching this idea to Animal Planet. If they give us the green light, production would begin in a few months. Do you think you'd be interested in a project like this?"

"Well yeah. Sure. I would be happy to give it some thought," I said, standing there in my underwear at 8 a.m. in the morning. I still hadn't had my first cup of coffee and a big shot director had called me out of thin air and asked if I wanted to star in his new TV show.

"You do realize I live in Missouri, don't you?" I asked.

"Oh that doesn't matter at all. We film all over the country. Look Gary, my team has done its research. We like what we've learned about you so far. To be honest, though, we are looking at two or three other people. Here's what we'd like you to do. Could you shoot a two or three minute video of yourself? I need to see something that captures the essence of who you are…something that will reveal a little bit more of your personality."

I said I could do that, and he said he needed the video by Thursday. "Pretty short notice, isn't it?" I kidded.

Then he said, "Gary, if we like the video, we'll fly you to Los Angeles for an audition. What do you think?"

To be honest, I was pretty blown away with all of this. Before I answered him, I took a sip of coffee and noticed the time. The clock said 8:12 a.m. I thought, "How incredible is this? My life might change forever from a 12 minute phone call."

"OK," I said. "I'll send it as soon as I can." We made some small talk about Steve Jobs and his new biography which we'd both just finished reading. Then he supplied me with his contact information and the address to forward the video to and that was that.

As soon as I hung up, I went to my computer and hurriedly checked out Todd Miller's bio. Indeed, he was a bona fide producer/director. I took a look at "My Cat from Hell," the show he'd produced. The show was in its fifth season and was a big hit.

I sat for a minute, letting all this info sink in for a moment. I got dressed and took the dogs for our morning hike. Along the trail I tried to weigh out the pros and cons of becoming a TV "Dog Whisperer." I knew if they selected me, my life would change drastically. Life as I know it now would never be the same again. Sure, it sounded glamorous, and I was flattered that I was being considered for the show.

Growing up in West Los Angeles, I became familiar with the entertainment industry at an early age. Many of the kids at the schools I attended were either actors themselves or their parents were. Some of the kids' parents were choreographers, make-up artists, set decorators, camera operators, stunt men, etc.

When I was nine years old, I begged my parents to allow me to audition for the lead role in the TV show "Dennis the Menace." They refused to drive me to the audition, and the role went to Jay North. Boy, was I pissed!

Three doors down from my house lived my friend Kevin Tate. One day he told me he was taking acting lessons and had an agent. Within six months he began appearing on television and eventually ended up working in the movies. I was so envious. Again I began working on my parents to let me take acting lessons. They steadfastly refused. There was going to be no "show biz" for little Gary.

In junior high I was surrounded by celebrities and some of them were quite famous. Later, at University High School my friends were people like David Cassidy and Cher's sister Georgianne LaPierre. The list of famous alumni at my school is really remarkable. Liz Taylor, Marilyn Monroe, Jeff Bridges, Barry Gordon, Dave Navarro, Nancy Sinatra, Randy Newman, Karla Bonoff. Remember Lynette "Squeaky" Fromm? The Charlie Manson cult member who tried to shoot President Ford? Yeah. She went there too. I marveled how they transformed my shy, skateboarding buddy David into David Cassidy, international megastar. I just couldn't believe that the guy I used to build forts and ride bikes with was now worshipped by just about every young teenage girl in the world. Yes, I learned early about Hollywood. The good and the bad.

So with that background in mind, I kept asking myself, "How will this benefit me? What are the positives and negatives? I knew that if the show was a hit, if it really took off, it might last three or four years. It would make me a pretty wealthy man. But at what cost? If I had to move back to LA, homes there cost a fortune. I would have no time to myself. There would be contracts to sign. They would own me. Personal appearances, people looking into my personal life. Would I have any creative input into the show or would everything be scripted? Oy vay! Too many decisions. The problem was Miller wanted that video right away.

All right, I decided. I'll do the video and it will just be fun to see if it gets me to the audition in California. I'd get a free trip and free meals. I could go to the beach and visit my friends. So, I called my good buddy Al Hillker and asked him if he would help me out. I explained to him what was going on and asked him if he'd video me "like right now!" He agreed to help and showed up at my house within the hour. Al was pretty excited about the whole thing. I had Al video me with my cellphone. Then he shot me walking around my horses while I talked about my work rehabilitating dogs. Later that day he accompanied me while I did a behavioral consultation at my client's house in Glendale. The video looked pretty good, I thought. I packaged up the video and emailed it to Miller in NYC.

I mentioned this to a couple of my closer friends and they were ecstatic. "Oh my God, Gary, this is big! You're going to be a star!"

"Whoa, wait a minute, hold on!" I said. "I seriously doubt I'll make it to the audition!"

"Oh yes you will," they all said enthusiastically. I just smiled at them. I knew not to get too excited. I was familiar with the old adage, "If it sounds too good to be true, it probably is." I knew I had a shot, but I am realistic. I'm well into my sixties, and I'm not all inked up and pierced like the star of Miller's "My Cat from Hell": Jackson Galoxy. Besides I live in the sticks in Missouri. Doesn't sound too sexy. But still, while I really had my doubts, I was excited thinking about it all.

I thought, even if I ended up being selected for the show, and even if it greatly disrupted my life, it would only be temporary. A couple of years at best, and I could walk away from it with several million dollars. It would no doubt be enough to buy a place by the ocean in the Redwoods.

A couple of days later, the phone rang and the screen said "New York City."

"Hey Gary. It's Todd Miller from Animal Planet. Got the video. I enjoyed it. It sure seems like you know your stuff. I've given the video to my team. I'll be back in touch with you soon.

A couple of days went by, then a couple of weeks. Soon a month had gone by, and I didn't hear from Animal Planet. I never heard from Todd Miller again.

A few days ago I looked to see if the show made it to production. It had. I checked to see who they had selected instead of me. They chose someone from Los Angeles whom I had never heard of. When I tried to find her online, it was obvious that they had "scrubbed" her from the internet. She was absolutely nowhere to be found. The show states the she had been training for 40 years, yet I couldn't find out anything about her. Curious. Oh well.

I guess they didn't like my pickup truck and cowboy hat.

Gary Abelov

Taming the Wild Child

A few days ago I was called to a client's home to help with her 10-month-old Golden Retriever. He was a friendly guy, just a young goofball, full of life, and bristling with energy. Just wanting to say "Hi!" he jumped on people at the front door, and he yanked his owner around while she attempted to walk him through the neighborhood. He also loved to grab socks and underwear and race through the house as if possessed.

My client had a few other minor complaints about her dog's behavior, but nothing that couldn't be fixed with a little time, practice and patience.

We were just about through with the session and were just sitting on the floor playing with Mr. Knucklehead, when somehow we got on the subject or anthropomorphism, or attributing human characteristics to animals. I mentioned that most dog lovers, including yours truly, did this all the time without being consciously aware of it. Just as I was about to explain myself, the Golden sneezed and my client said "Gesundheit!" We both laughed, and I said, "See what I mean?" Later I told this story to a friend who just happened to speak affluent German. "Do you know what "Gesundheit" means?" she asked. Gesundheit, it happens, means good health. And that got me thinking about a favorite topic – the role of exercise in maintaining a dog's health.

When a dog runs through your house as if it has been stung in the rear by a bee, or when your pal knocks people down or just jumps all over them, more than likely he is not getting sufficient exercise. His aerobic requirements are probably not being met. If you really want your dog to be calm and well-behaved, if you want a healthy dog – a Gesundheit Dog – start exercising your dog daily.

The working, hunting, and sporting dogs are bred for endurance and work. While very few of these breeds actually do what they are bred to do, they still need lots of daily aerobic activity. How many Golden and Labrador Retrievers are there in the St. Louis area? How many hunt? Almost none! They might not be hunting as they were intended to do, but they still need an outlet for all their energy.

Kane, my German Shepherd, doesn't have a flock to herd, but he still has all that working dog energy inside him that needs to come out one way or another. For all of our dogs, for good health, and to solve most unruliness problems, daily exercise is critically important. It is also an extremely important factor in the bonding process between you and your friend. Your backyard is not going to provide your canine with exercise. Even if you have a huge yard or live in the country, turning your friend outside for an hour or two will give your dog virtually no exercise at all. Oh he might chase a squirrel or two and fence fight with the neighbor's dog, but this provides virtually no real exercise for your little triathlete.

I've listened to thousands upon thousands of dog lovers saying something like this: "We have a gigantic fenced yard. If she wants to run around, she has all the room in the world. So if she chooses not to run, I guess she doesn't need to run or she would." That kind of thinking causes a lot of problems. Dogs think differently than we do. They simply won't go out into the yard and think, "I gotta get in shape. Think I'll do some laps and then maybe some pushups and a few pull-ups." They will most likely walk around a little, make sure nobody has been in their yard, do some sniffing around, then walk back to the door or lie down in the shade somewhere.

Do you know that only 10 per cent of dog guardians walk their dogs on a regular basis? I'm not kidding. It's always the same folks out there with their dogs every day walking through the neighborhood. If every dog in the St. Louis City and County were being walked every day, you wouldn't have room to drive down the street to work.

Daily walking will do it for most dogs, but for the really high energy types, jogging, fetch, swimming, Frisbee or fly ball might be more helpful. If your dog comes back inside and is still a little wound up, then on the next walk try walking a bit longer, say five or 10 minutes more. Do this daily, year round, and I promise your dog's behavior and health will improve dramatically.

Swatch

List of problems from Swatch's guardian:

- Tears up toys
- Grabs anything – shoes, socks, thread, food
- Constantly has something in her mouth
- Reaches cabinets, counter tops, tables
- Digs along fence/house
- Eats anything: acorns, sticks, dog poop, and flower petals.
- I can't let her out of my sight.
- Jumps on people and pulls on clothes.
- Aggressive with food when other dogs are around
- Hard to walk. Pulls.
- Wild with other people
- Runs along fence

Gary Abelov

The Executive

The dog's name was Rusty. He was a big, silly, young and handsome Golden Retriever. He was also a dog with more than a few behavioral issues. His loving guardian was the CEO of a large, well-known corporation in St. Louis. "Gary, as you know, I have well over a thousand employees, and they, of course, listen to me. But Rusty doesn't give a damn what I tell him to do. I really need your help."

Ted, the executive and dog lover went on to say, "In fact, I need your help as quickly as possible; how soon can you come? "

I met Ted and Rusty the next day at his stately mansion near the Bogey Club in St. Louis's exclusive Ladue suburb. Rusty greeted me with great excitement. Ted's greeting was more dignified, but warm and gracious. We sat in the kitchen in front of a stone fireplace 10 feet wide and so high I could have stood inside without bumping my head.

As we drank coffee together, Ted reminded me that he wasn't used to anyone – human or dog – not listening to him. Rusty positioned himself in front of the fireplace and watched us carefully. I pointed at Rusty and laughed. "He looks like he's smirking at you, Ted."

"He looks at me like that all the time," said Ted.

I soon learned that Ted had recently remarried, and his new wife was not a dog lover. She was someone who liked to hold catered barbeques. Rusty enjoyed a party as much as the next dog, but his party manners lacked finesse. He was, in fact, a dedicated crotch and butt sniffer, and he preferred women. Rusty's specialty was butting a female backside hard enough to scoot the victim several feet across the floor. If the men at the barbeque were well lubricated with beer and cocktails, they roared with laughter whenever Rusty engaged in his "specialty."

After Paula's second barbeque, she began insisting Ted "do something" about his dog.

Then came the pool party. While guests were in the pool, Rusty ran along the sides of the pool barking incessantly. A few of guests thought they might discourage Rusty by splashing water at him. This approach failed miserably. Rusty loved being splashed. He snapped at the splashed water. FUN! Pleased that these humans wanted to play, Rusty jumped in the pool. Unfortunately, Rusty was not a natural swimming. His backend sank, and he began thrashing about and attempting to climb on top of any human he thought might save him. Since Ted hated clipping Rusty's toe nails, those long nails were now slicing into the unfortunate objects of Rusty's frantic attention. Finally, Ted managed to rescue his dog from the pool. Rusty returned to running around the edge of the pool while barking his head off.

Finally, someone escorted Rusty to the house and shut him inside where he howled his displeasure. Since the barking seemed more annoying that the swimming pool escapades, Rusty gained his freedom again and decided to concentrate on his "specialty," sniffing and butting as many female guests as possible.

And this was the dog who now seemed to be smirking at me, just daring me to interfere with his chosen lifestyle. I accepted the challenge.

I worked with Ted and Rusty once a week for six weeks. With training, self-control exercises, daily walks, some rules and boundaries, Rusty's behavior really improved.

About a year later, Ted suddenly passed away. Amazingly, Paula didn't immediately give Rusty the boot. He had matured quite a bit since I had first met him. He was still a big goof, but he had matured and was a smart and very handsome boy. Paula hadn't suddenly turned into a dog person, but Rusty did have a friend. Ted's assistant, Mary, lived on the estate and loved Rusty as much as he loved her. Whenever Paula was out of town (which was often because she spent a lot of time in Aspen and a couple months every year in Europe), Mary gave Rusty the full run of the house and even let him sleep on her bed.

One day I received a call from Paula. She asked me to come back to the house and show her where to put the invisible fence that was soon to be installed. Truth is, I never really liked Paula. Ted was a dog lover and a hell of a nice guy, but Paula disliked dogs and was snooty, sarcastic and generally negative.

So anyway, Mary, Paula and I walked around the estate and I explained where the fence should go and why. I advised against running the fence up to the street, but Paula argued with everything I suggested. As I left, she said she would send me a check for my services. It never arrived. I guess it was lost in the mail.

A couple months later, Mary called to tell me that Paula had done exactly what I asked her not to do and brought the fence line right up to the road. One day a group of ladies were walking along the lane with their dogs. Rusty ran excitedly along the fence line, barking wildly, and working himself up into such a frenzy that he ran through the fence line and got into a fight with one of the dogs. The women were able to stop the fight, but not before someone got bitten.

Paula decided that Rusty was "out of here." Mary was heartbroken but couldn't talk Paula out of her decision.

Then one day I answered a call from some people who wanted help with the Golden Retriever they'd just adopted. His name was Rusty. Well, a lot of Golden Retrievers are named Rusty.

When I arrived for my appointment, I was shocked to meet my old pal. Yup, Rusty from Ladue. Ted's dog. Rusty sniffed, recognized my voice and then gave me quite a greeting.

My new client asked, "Do you know each other?"

It was obvious we did.

Gary Abelov

A Few Observations

For every 50 telephone inquiries I receive from women, I receive only two or three from men.

Dog lovers too often do not like to walk or train their dogs. Approximately two per cent of St. Louis dog guardians walk their dogs daily. Only about one percent actually train their dogs to any appreciative level.

Almost everyone is afraid to clip their dog's nails.

The majority of dog lovers seem to prefer the company of their dogs to that of humans. Don't believe me, just ask them.

I have never met a dog that is afraid of women.

Adult dogs sleep about 60 percent of the time.

Most dog guardians fail to establish clear rules or boundaries for their dogs. I've been told over and over, "I don't want my dog to think I'm mean or too strict. I know I should stop giving in to him. I don't want him to be unhappy.

Dog lovers tell me, "The reason my dog won't listen to me is because she's so stubborn. Actually, dogs always listen. They sometimes just won't comply with our requests. Lack of training is probably the real reason your dog blows you off. Also, some dogs are so used to doing anything they want, they have little tolerance for frustration. In other words, they live to please themselves and can't handle taking direction from their human. When dogs won't "listen," ask yourself, "Why should he?" Dog breeds all vary in their level of working intelligence. The brightest dogs can learn new tasks quickly. They will also accept your direction from a good distance. Dogs that are not bred to work learn much more slowly and from a distance probably won't listen at all. The process of training a dog conditions them to respond to you, even though they might not really want to.

People usually feel guilty about crating their dogs, so they go overboard in trying to make the crate "comfy" by stuffing the crate with many layers of bedding. They figure that's what they would want. Not really. Dogs sweat through the pads of their feet. They can become uncomfortable in overly padded crates.

Dogs are not as emotionally fragile as people generally think they are. Dogs can handle adversity and pain quite well. While an abrupt change in their daily routine can be unsettling, they can usually roll with it.

Many dog lovers believe that dogs go to the bathroom in the house out of spite and anger.

A significant number of the clients I work with believe their dogs dislike black people. They quietly and discreetly ask me if it's their smell.

A significant number of the clients I work with believe their dogs dislike white people. They quietly and discreetly ask me if it's their smell.

Dogs hate cigarette smoke, rain, and gloomy days. Our crying also seems to upset them.

All dogs will quickly respond to the sound of a crinkling treat bag.

"Wanna go for a walk?" and "Wanna go for a ride?" are universally wonderful questions to dogs.

The majority of dog people will try to stop their dog from sniffing another dog's butt or a visitor's crotch. They think it's impolite, but it is, in fact, normal dog behavior. Can't we just let dogs be dogs?

Not Such a Good Idea

- Buying a young energetic puppy for an elderly parent (Wouldn't an old slow dog be better?)
- Buying a dog to give as a present
- Buying a dog from an unknown breeder – especially one that you found online
- Buying a dog (puppy) when you are rarely at home due to work or social activities
- Going camping or traveling with a newly adopted or purchased dog
- Buying a dog and immediately dragging it around to all of your friends and relatives homes. Equally bad is inviting everyone you know over to meet your new dog.
- Buying a second dog to help ease your new dog's separation anxiety.
- Letting a breeder insist that you not spay or neuter your new dog.
- Relying on punishment and "discipline" to teach a dog appropriate behaviors. After all, you have to show your dog who is the boss or alpha? Right? Wrong!
- Thinking you can solve your dog's behavior problems with a few phone calls to friends, family and dog trainers. Problem behaviors cannot be diagnosed over the phone.
- Buying a high energy puppy when you have a new baby, thinking it will be wonderful to watch them grow up together. Most new moms have absolutely no idea how much work, time, love and patience a growing puppy needs. For nearly a year, puppies are pooping, peeing, chewing, mischief-making machines. For 30 years, women have told me that puppies are more work that human children.

- Buying a dog from any pet store and most website breeders. Pet store puppies almost always come from puppy mills. No Matter What The Store Managers Tell You! Save yourself the heartache and trouble!

- Buying from newspaper ads and Craig's List. Trust me. These places area dumping grounds for amateur breeders. Quality breeders never sell in these places just as they never sell to pet stores. Quality breeders carefully screen buyers and match puppies with the lifestyles of the buyers and their families. High quality puppies are reserved with a deposit six months to a year before they are born. If you must have a purebred dog, please do your homework. You will have to live with your decision for many years. How do you find good puppies? Call your local (breed of your choice) club and ask then who sells the healthiest dogs. When you call a breeder, ask them for referrals (at least 10) and call them! Also, ask for the name of the breeder's veterinarian and call the vet too. A great breeder will not be offended when being asked for referrals. On the contrary, they are proud of their dogs and the way they are bred and raised.

- Buying an active young dog if you have an elderly dog. Good Lord! The pup will jump on, nip at and generally make your senior dog miserable. No, puppies don't give your senior a "new lease on life." Let your old dog enjoy its remaining days on earth in peace.

Quickies

- Riley the Golden Retriever brought me his mom's vibrator while I was training his friend.
- Lulu, the Shepherd mix, could open the refrigerator door and bring cans of beer to guests.
- One dog ate his mom's wedding ring, not once but twice.
- Rex the Golden Retriever mix dragged a deer's head through the dog door and placed in on the living room couch.
- Nick the Yellow Labrador Retriever chewed through an apartment wall. When the neighbor walked into his kitchen, Nick's head was all the way through the wall, barking at the stunned stranger.
- Luna the Weimaraner stole nine potatoes from the pantry and hid them all over the house.
- A woman had five Yorkshire Terriers who repeatedly fought on top of her while she slept. When I suggested she might just remove the dogs from her bed, she sobbed uncontrollably.
- Moose the feral dog escaped from his new home (kids left gate open). It took about 30 people a full week to catch him. While on the loose, Moose covered about 15 miles, swam across the River Des Peres twice, and was hit twice by cars. He also bit the rescuer who tackled him. In spite of this unlikely beginning, Moose became – over time – a wonderful, loving family member.
- Kane the German Shepherd chewed and completely destroyed four Native American/Kachina Dolls valued at over $10,000.
- Apache the Australian Shepherd not only ate coins and underwear but also devoured a gold chain and dad's dentures.

- Ben and Jerry, a pair of pugs, humped each other constantly. Their owners showed me a video to prove their point. I suggested that they erase the "doggy porn video."
- Drake "air humped" whenever he heard the beep of a car's horn.
- Billy the Rhodesian Ridgeback ripped into his owners oil paints and covered his legs, face and chest in red and yellow paint. He also managed to squish the paint over the floor and elsewhere throughout the house. Billy had to be completely shaved since the oil paints couldn't be washed away.
- Mama the nursing home dog was one seriously obese dog. She routinely visited the residents' rooms. If the resident didn't offer her treats, she stole them.
- Misha was trained to pee in the toilet. If I hadn't seen it with my own eyes, I wouldn't have believed it possible. She would lift the toilet lid, hop on the seat, squat and pee. The only thing she couldn't do was flush, but her guardian was teaching her that next.
- Clients claimed that their Border Collie would sit at the side of their bed and watch them make love. They swore he never sat by the bed at any other time. They said he always had a "grin" on his face.
- Bradley the Rottweiler would hold the cat down with his front paws and lick its head and back until it fell asleep. Once kitty was fast asleep, Bradley would get up and walk away.
- A Labrador Retriever jumped out of a second floor window, ran into the street and was immediately struck by a car. She broke several bones and was in bad shape for quite a while. A year later, she jumped out of the same window, breaking several more bones. Her guardians asked me to help them before their lab killed herself.

- A client with an unruly dog once asked me to join him in prayer before we began our session. We bowed our heads and as he prayed, I opened one eye and saw his cat stand on its hind legs, place its front paws on the sofa's edge, and squirt loose a large pile of diarrhea. I've always wondered if this incident in any way diminished my client's faith in the power of prayer.

- Nikki, a large Rottweiler, had a problem with the mail carrier. Every day, as the carrier brought the mail to the slot on the porch, Nikki jumped on the oval glass window in the center of the front door. This continued until one day Nikki hit the glass with such force that it shattered and she exploded through the opening. The terrified mail carrier froze, expecting the worst. But much to the carrier's relief, Nikki approached with a wagging tail. She seemed to think she and the carrier were the best of friends.

Why Not Adopt?

As an alternative to buying from a breeder, please consider adopting. I have five wonderful dogs lying at my feet as I write this. They are all happy, healthy, beautiful, and all are from a local shelter. Let me say this: I adopted my gorgeous big German Shepherd, Kane, when he was only ten months old. Great dog! He loves everyone. He came neutered, heartworm tested, all shots current, micro-chipped. I paid $125 for him. I could easily have paid $3,000 for the same dog from a breeder. Don't be afraid to go to a shelter to look. Rescue groups are also a great place to look for dogs.

If you must buy a dog from a breeder, please, please be careful. Amateur breeders all too often sell poorly socialized dogs with an endless list of health problems. Not a week goes by that I'm not called to see a dog with fear-related problems. "Hobby" breeders frequently advertise in the classified section of the Sunday paper. Sincere, quality breeders virtually never sell pups through the newspaper or on Craig's List. Avoid these places at all costs.

Naturally, inexperienced breeders and puppy mills sell dogs over the internet. I have purposely looked at the websites of some of the most notorious commercial dog breeding operations. They have beautiful photographs of fat, healthy-looking dogs romping on lush green lawns. These very same breeders have been cited repeatedly by various authorities for the horrific living conditions of their dogs.

Another place you will want to avoid is pet stores. Perhaps 50 years ago you could pick up puppies at a local "mom and pop" pet store and not have to worry about their temperament or health. Today, all pet stores buy from brokers who buy their puppies from puppy mills. There are never, ever any exceptions. Pet stores depend on these horrible places to supply them with the pups they sell. My clients have bought puppies at pet stores and have had endless problems with them. Oh my god! Hearing and vision problems. Joints and hips that don't work. Digestive problems. Parasites. Allergies. The list goes on. Fear issues abound, as these puppies have had virtually no human contact until they arrive at the store, where the contact is limited and usually too late.

When I gently asked my clients why they bought a dog at the mall, they usually reply, "It was an impulse buy." Or they'll say they called some breeders but nobody had any puppies at the time, so they went to the puppy store at the mall.

If you want to buy your dog from a breeder, DO YOUR HOMEWORK! Especially check references. Visit the breeder's home. A huge red flag is when the breeder won't let you visit their home or kennel. Never buy a puppy unless you can visit with BOTH of the puppy's parents. If the breeder wants to meet you at a truck stop on the interstate or at a McDonalds, Run!

There are thousands of purebred rescue groups all over the United States. And I understand that more than 30 percent of the dogs waiting for homes in animal shelters are purebred dogs.

Finally, consider adopting a senior dog. I used to buy puppies thinking that I could mold and shape them as they matured, and I did. However, I have found such joy in bringing older dogs into my home, into my life. They don't chew. They're housebroken (usually). And they are ever so grateful for a second chance.

Hi-Pointe

About a year ago I received a call from a man who said, "I think we have met our match, Gary." We've had dogs for many, many years, but our new dog is definitely a piece of work. We need help!"

Nothing unusual about a request like this. I get them every day. It's just that this call came while I was still in bed and half asleep. Usually Angie, my Shepherd mix and matriarch of my dog family, wakes me up very early. For some reason, she "slept in" than morning. I was a little startled when the phone rang on the night stand about a foot from my head.

The man went on to say, "Our dog's name is Gracie. She's chewed everything in our house. A couple of remote controls, shoes, furniture, and this morning she ate my wife's new prescription glasses."

"I think I can help you. What breed dog is Gracie, do you know?" I asked.

He went on talking about Gracie while I got out of bed and found my way downstairs to my desk. I began to write down all the particulars and assured him that everything would be fine.

I'll admit I am actually relieved when I get "easy" cases like this. Destructive chewing is not difficult to resolve. It is nice not to have to deal with complex issues for a change. I just needed to show up at my client's house, explain the "whys" of the dog's chewing and the "how's" of fixing the problem. A consultation like this generally takes about an hour and a half.

However, a seemingly routine consultation can became anything but routine in a matter of moments. My clients, the Benjamans, lived near an independent movie house called the Hi-Pointe where at the tender age of 15, I'd watched my first double feature, a pair of erotic films totally inappropriate for a kid my age. I'd walked out of that theater in a state of profound shock. I was about to experience a jolt of a different sort at the Benjaman's.

Gracie the one-year-old chewing Labrador met me at the door. She was happy, happy, happy to have company, jumping all over me and showering me with kisses. "We just love her. We know she's still very young, and we get that. We just have to figure out a way to get her to stop chewing."

I asked few questions. "Does your dog go for walks? How often?" I continued: "Tell me about the items she has destroyed."

Just then someone knocked on the door, and Mrs. Benjaman found herself facing a police officer. Within seconds, the officer and both Benjamans walked down the hallway. "Excuse us, Gary," she said. "I need to see what the hell is going on."

I'm used to interruptions. It's a constant when I make house calls, but I had never yet had the police walk in on a consultation.

So while the Benjamans talked with the police officer, I played with Gracie, looked around at the family portraits and checked my cellphone for messages.

After a few minutes, a young girl (maybe 13 or 14) walked into the living room with tears in her eyes and her hands handcuffed behind her back. Walking behind her was the police officer and the Benjamans who, believe me, did not look happy.

"Gary, I'm so sorry but we're going to have to cancel our consultation," Mrs. Benjaman said.

I couldn't get out of that little scene fast enough. I let myself out the door and watched the cop open the back door of his squad car and help the Benjaman's daughter sit down. I had absolutely no idea what had just happened. I left shocked and a little shaken. Jesus, that was really strange.

A few days later, Mrs. Benjaman called me again.

"I just want to say how sorry and embarrassed we are." She went on to explain what caused the arrest of her daughter. Apparently their daughter, who had never been in any trouble before, has been bullied at school for several months. On the morning I visited their home, the daughter, Erin, was once again on the receiving end of a bully's taunts. She was in the hallway in front of her class, talking to a friend and eating a pastry when her bully approached her, made some nasty remarks, and then pushed the pastry in Erin's face.

That's all it took. Erin had had enough. She hauled off and punched the bully in the mouth. Her punch caught her tormentor off guard and Erin laid into her with more punches. A teacher heard the commotion and had to pull Erin away from the bully. Erin received a three day suspension as did the other girl.

That might have been the end of it, but the bully girl's mother was livid. Her daughter's version of the story was that Erin was the bully and had attacked for no reason at all. Naturally, mom was outraged and called the police. Erin's arrest took place while I was at the Benjaman's home.

After the police investigated the incident further, they were satisfied that Erin was indeed the victim of bullying. They did not file any charges.

The following week I returned to see Gracie and the Benjamans again. This time there was a "lightness" in the air. Erin apologized to me and I told her, "There is nothing to be sorry about. In fact, I'm proud of you. You stood your ground and defended yourself."

With that, she smiled and gave me a big hug.

Then we all turned to Gracie, who'd never stopped being happy and would soon stop chewing up shoes, furniture, remote controls and glasses,

Gary Abelov

A Dog's Life

I live with five dogs in an old log house in the country. Every day before I go off to work, Kane, Angle, Rex, Sparky and Grover and I go hiking in the heavily wooded hills that surround the homestead.

Today as I was poking around the forest floor looking for arrow heads, I found a really nice old deer antler. It was all bleached out but was still in pretty good condition. Cool! I have found several others over the years, and now I could add this one to the collection.

One by one the dogs came up to me to see what I was doing, and I showed them my newfound treasure. Each sniffed it, except for Sparky, my Dalmatian mix. He tried to chew on it. Kane, my German Shepherd, seemed not impressed at all and just looked at it briefly before trotting ahead toward the creek. When I caught up with Kane a few minutes later, he was standing above the creek on a steep hill looking directly at me. Normally Kane is not one for prolonged eye contact, but today he was staring straight into my eyes. He was looking at me with what I call "smiling eyes." You know how people look at you when they are in possession of some happy information and they are just bursting at the seams to tell you? That's the way Kane was looking at me.

As I was walking toward him, I laughed and said, "What?" He looked away from my eyes and down at the ground in front of him. There at his feet were some deer hide fragments, deer ribs, and to my amazement, a deer antler. My jaw dropped as I compared it to the one I had found a few minutes earlier. It was an obvious match! Kane had seen me showing off my deer antler and knew that I valued it. So when he found the other bones, he told me through eye contact, "Look here. Here's more!"

As I walked back home holding my deer antlers, I thought about what I learned from Kane today. I was reminded how effectively dogs can communicate with each other and with the people in their lives.

Dogs are so real and without pretense. Dogs truly stop to smell the flowers all the time. They wake up at the crack of dawn and happily look forward to another day.

It really is a dog's life, isn't it? Sure, they don't live as long as we do, but they don't fret about how long they'll live or worry about finances or illness. They sure as hell don't worry about their appearance or about fat and cholesterol, do they?

If you have some time today, take your friend for a walk or just hang out in the backyard or park together. I'll bet you learn something, even if it's just a friendly reminder from your best friend to slow down forget your troubles for a little while and just enjoy each other and the moment.

The Egg Timer

Anyone in the dog training business spends a lot of time on the phone. Potential clients will call day and night. "What do you charge?" is of course one of the most common questions, along with "Where are you located?" and "Do you make house calls?" Many ask for references and credentials and inquire about dog training methods.

Whatever the reason for a call, I have a tendency to talk too much. Realizing this, I once decided to put a time limit on each call I received. To help me with this, I bought an old-fashioned egg timer, and set it for 12 minutes.

The egg timer was a great idea in theory. Then I received my first call after putting the timer next to my phone. I had a nice conversation with the woman on the other end of the line, answering her questions about my fees and availability. Then BING, the egg time went off. The woman immediately asked me if I was timing her. I replied with a laugh, and nervously replied, "No. No. No. Don't be silly." I considered saying I was boiling an egg but thought I might be pushing my luck there. I could tell she wasn't happy. But she did hire me anyway. I wondered if she would bring up the egg timer when I went to her house, but she didn't.

I took the egg timer to another room so people couldn't hear it. About a month later, I threw it away.

Gary Abelov

Call Log

- Daughter divorced, now living in basement of parents' house. Her dog fights with parents' dog.
- Call from Lake of their Ozarks. Need phone consultation. Potty training.
- Request for intermediate training. St. Charles
- Fearful dog, just adopted
- Unruly dog. Won't allow nails to be clipped, chases cat. Steals food from kitchen counter.
- Request from rescue group. Dog boarded in kennel waiting for foster. Dog is "hyper," not fond of other dogs, especially females.

Gary Abelov

Exotic Clientele

With her whispery voice, she sounded like a young girl. "I'm uh having some big problems with my dog. My dog's doctor suggested I call you."

Apparently she had a six month old puppy who was not yet potty trained. He was also chewing up stuff and jumping on her and everyone else. We decided to meet the following Monday at noon.

The young lady lived in a "cracker box" house with a carport in an old neighborhood where most of the streets were named for saints – Saint Mary, Saint Christopher, etc. Benny the dog was not quite ready for sainthood. When I walked in, he jumped all over me, spun in circles and raced around the room. He had plenty of room, too, because the living room contained not a stick of furniture.

I set my equipment bag and briefcase on the ground, and settled down, brushing off her apologies about the lack of furniture. My client, Teri, joined me on the floor. To say she was pretty would be almost an insult to her incredible beauty. She was 21 or 22 and well, distracting in her short shorts and tank top. Then to my surprise and pleasure, two more equally beautiful young women joined us. Teri introduced her sisters Amanda and Tracie. So there I was sitting in a circle with three scantily-dressed drop-dead gorgeous young women. And we were talking about housebreaking a puppy. Sigh.

I asked about their work schedules and learned that all three worked in Illinois and drove to and from work together, leaving about 5 p.m. and getting back around 3 a.m.

Innocently, I asked if they worked together. After a short pause, while all three must have thought I was a country rube, Amanda, with a smile, said, "We are dancers."

Ah. I'm a little slow, but I put the pieces together. Late hours. Really cute. Illinois. Got it. Exotic dancers. Strippers. I tried to act casual.

"That's cool," I said.

Teri must have felt the need to explain things. "We had a very bad childhood, Gary. Our dad was a mean drunk. He abused us verbally and physically. Our mom tried to stop the abuse, but she was as terrified of him as we were. After we graduated high school, we left home and scraped up enough money to rent a crappy little roach and mouse infested apartment." Amanda added, "But we were happy. We felt free for the first time in our lives."

Later, they were homeless for a while, crashing at different people's homes or sleeping in their van. "But happy," Amanda emphasized again. "Hungry, but happy."

I quietly listened on.

"It took about a year, but with all of us working, we were able to put down a security deposit and the money for the first and last month's rent," Tracie said.

"We began dancing," Tracie said, "because we could make good money quickly. A year and a half ago I got pregnant and gave birth to my daughter." Her eyes lit up as she asked, "Wanna see her? She's sleeping right now. C'mon. Come see!"

We tiptoed into the nursery. Her daughter slept in her crib. Unlike the rest of the house, the nursery was full of furniture, with walls decorated with angels and unicorns.

As mom and the sisters looked at the sleeping baby, their formerly solemn faces changed. Now everyone was smiling. It was as if in this room and around the baby, all was right with the world.

We walked back into the living room and settled back on the floor. As I played with their dog a little, they offered me a soda and I answered their dog training questions. Somehow the conversation turned to furniture, or rather to their homes lack thereof. Teri said they had just purchased a couch, a kitchen table and chairs, new beds and a coffee table. They were disappointed that I had come before the furniture was delivered.

Amanda then informed me that their next goal was to enroll as students at Florissant Community College only a mile or two from their home. I was impressed.

I concluded that these beautiful young women were really strong people. Obviously they loved each other and were proud of how they had survived their troubled childhood. They were making their own way as adults. I trusted them to follow through with their college plans and their puppy's training.

Before I left that afternoon, Tracie invited me to see them dance at the club where they performed. Hell, they even gave me a handful of free passes and some "free drink" cards. I thanked them profusely and told them I would come see them soon, but I knew I wouldn't. I liked them too much.

Gary Abelov

Thistle

List of problems from Thistle's guardian:

- Has bitten and broken the skin three times. Has bitten countless people on their ankles and lower legs.
- Hates other dogs
- Afraid of thunder storms.
- Sometimes barks at his dog bowl for no apparent reason (even when full of food).
- Goes crazy in the car
- Pulls on his leash when walking. Sometimes will not get in the car and if I pick him up, he growls and snaps at me

Gary Abelov

Bruno

The rain was really starting to get on my nerves. I can handle a day or two of rain, but that's about it. I once lived in the Redwoods by the ocean and it rained all the time. Not uncommon for it to pour nonstop for up to 20 days straight. After three years, there, I had developed a supreme dislike for rain.

It had been raining hard for four days, so hard that my cedar shake roof was beginning to leak. Finally the rain began to let up and the sun was beginning to shire. Hallelujah! I knew it would be a muddy mess outside, but the dogs were going stir crazy, so I took them for a hike. The dogs seem to hate the rain as much as I do. They were so damn happy to get out of the house and run through the woods. I knew that I had an appointment that afternoon with "an increasingly aggressive dog," so the hike had to be a little shorter than usual. I needed plenty of time to review the notes from my phone conversation with the new clients and to get to their home. What I knew was that Bruno was a male boxer mix, 80 pounds, adopted five months ago. The client was afraid to walk him because he pulled hard and barked at strangers. He also barked at visitors to their home. He hadn't bitten anyone, but the client was concerned.

When I arrived, my client was working in her front yard garden. I talked with her while getting my first look at Bruno as he raced back and forth behind the backyard picket fence, barking hysterically. My presence clearly agitated him. He was a big dog with a Boxer's face but a long, lanky body and skinny legs. My client, Corrine, looked nervous. "How do you want to do this?" she asked. We decided that I would go inside and she would put a leash on Bruno and bring him inside to meet me. Once inside with my equipment bag and briefcase, I noticed that the door to the kitchen was blocked by a card table turned on its side. Piles of books on each side of the table held it in place. I'd seen this before many times. Instead of buying a real gate, people will improvise with card tables, plywood, lattice panels, bricks, books and furniture. Usually these makeshift arrangements work for a while. But puppies quickly grow bigger and stronger, and soon they push through the barrier.

I suddenly heard Bruno running across the kitchen floor. Making a whining sound, he slid into the card table gate and with his nose easily pushed it out of the way. Before I could react, he raced straight for me, leaped up and hit me with such force that he knocked me over. I struck the back of my head on the leg of the dining room table. I had almost made it to my feet when he came at me again. I stumbled backwards and tripped over a box, fell and hit my head on the wall. I didn't lose consciousness, but I was pretty dazed. Bruno was now on top of me and not interested in making friends. The first bite was on my shoulder, the second my chest. I desperately tried to right myself and protect my body at the same time. I was able to grab my equipment bag and hold in in front of my stomach and chest. Bruno started biting the bag. I could hear Corrine screaming, and I mean screaming. "What should I do!? What should I do!?" I yelled back, "Get him off me! Get a leash on him!"

As she pulled Bruno back, I struggled to stand upright. Bruno was still lunging at me and barking uncontrollably, saliva spraying everywhere. Corrine was hysterical and holding a death grip on Bruno's leash as he gradually ceased barking and lunging. I managed to take a couple of deep breaths and check my wounds. I found several puncture wounds and some bleeding, but remarkably nothing more serious. My head really hurt and a huge lump had formed at the back of my head, but I was still among the living. I excused myself to clean my wounds. When I returned to the living room, Corrine was still hysterical and Bruno began lunging at me again.

Ordinarily I would now help fit the dog with a head collar. It takes me about 25 seconds to do it myself. But if the dog does not take kindly to strangers, I need to talk the client through the procedure. This is difficult under the best of circumstances. But when the dog has just attacked someone and the owner is emotionally shaken, the job is close to impossible. Corrine's hands were trembling, and she was on the verge of tears as she closely followed my instructions. One wrong move, one slip, and Bruno could have come after me again. Corrine managed to fit the head halter and could now connect the leash to the ring hanging below his chin.

I held my breath as she removed the leash from Bruno's collar and hooked it to the head collar. There! Done! With everything in place, she now had real control of her dog. Few people could have done what she'd done under such intense pressure.

Corrine was still shaking as she asked me, "What am I going to do? I love him, but I can't have this! I'm so sorry, Gary. I'm so sorry." Corrine must have apologized a dozen times or more. "Can we fix this? Is there any hope? I'm so scared."

Corrine went on to explain what had happened. Apparently as she walked into the backyard to get Bruno, he bolted just as she was going to attach the leash to the ring on his collar. He ran through the back door into the kitchen and then, well, you know the rest.

We walked outside to the street with Bruno, who was now in his newly fitted head collar and was more sedate. I showed Corrine how to hold the leash and how the head collar worked to control her dog. I asked her to hand me the leash. You should have seen the look on her face. She looked at me as if to say, "Are you crazy?" What she actually said was "Are you sure it's O.K" "Yeah," I replied, trying not to show the fear rising inside me.

We took several steps with me holding the leash. Bruno finally turned to look at me -- and instantly lunged. I was able to hold him at bay by sliding my left hand down the leash towards his head. I kept my arm out in a straight line. I "stiff armed" him until he stopped lunging and we continued our walk. Watching all this, Corrine got all wound up again and started crying. "What am I going to do?" She peppered me with questions as we walked through her neighborhood. About this time, my bites really starting to hurt and my head! Oh my God, did I have a headache!

Corrine was still shaken, but the walk and the nice weather had a calming effect on us all, including Cujo, aka Bruno. We walked for 20 minutes or so without incident and headed back to her home.

Back at her house, I gave the leash to Corrine and we sat down to talk. I explained that in cases of serious aggression like this, safety was of paramount importance. I tried to be honest and reassuring. "We can do many things. It is possible that we can turn him around, but there is no guarantee we will succeed. If she were to euthanize Bruno, no one would blame her.

Corrine told me that she would like to try to help him. "If we can't turn him around, at least I will think that I gave him every chance to be successful."

We spoke for an hour or so. My head was killing me and it was getting late. We talked about how we were going to approach Bruno's problems. Corrine was still upset as she escorted me to the door, and I said good-by to her and Bruno.

The following day I was down at the barn feeding my horses when my cellphone rang. It was Corrine. She called to tell me how terribly sorry she was that Bruno had attacked me and how responsible she felt for what had happened. She also told me through tears that she had decided to "put Bruno to sleep." She cried for a few seconds or more. "I love him so much, but I just can't risk him ever attacking someone again. I can't take him to a shelter. Who would take him? No, Gary, I couldn't live with myself if he hurt anyone."

I told Corrine that I understood what a hard decision this was to make and how much I respected her and supported her decision.

In my line of work, so matter how hard we try, we just can't save them all. Every dog trainer learns this eventually. It's one of the hardest lessons to learn and to accept.

Rest in peace, Bruno.

Training Guide Dogs.

Scout – My Hero.

Gary Abelov

Starry Night Publishing

Everyone has a story...

Don't spend your life trying to get published! Don't tolerate rejection! Don't do all the work and allow the publishing comp reap the rewards!

Millions of independent authors like you, are making mo publishing their stories now. Our technological know-how w the headaches out of getting published. Let "Starry Night Publishing dot Com" take care of the hard parts, so you can writing. You simply send us your Word document and we rest. It really is that simple!

The big companies want to publish only "celebrity au the average book-writer. It's almost impossible for first-t to get published today. This has led many authors to go t publishing route. Until recently, this was considered "va publishing." You spent large sums of your money, to g copies of your book, to give to relatives at Christmas, could see your name on the cover. Now, however, th publishing industry allows authors to get published i fashion, retain the rights to your work, keeping up t of your royalties, instead of the traditional ten-perc

We've opened up the gates, allowing you inside the world of publishing. While others charge you as much as ten-thousand dollars for a publishing package, we charge less than three-hundred dollars to cover proofreading, copyright, ISBN, and distribution costs. Do you really want to spend all your time formatting, converting, designing a cover, and then promoting your book, because no one else will?

Our editors are professionals, able to create a top-notch book that you will be proud of. Becoming a published author is supposed to be fun, not a hassle.

At Starry Night Publishing, you submit your work, we proofread it, create a professional-looking cover, a table of contents, compile your text and images into the appropriate format, convert your files for eReaders, take care of copyright information, assign an ISBN, allow you to keep one-hundred-percent of your rights, distribute your story worldwide on Amazon, Barnes & Noble and many other retailers, and write you a check for your royalties. There are no other hidden fees involved! You don't pay extra for a cover, or proofreading. You will never pay to keep your book in print. We promise! Everything is included! You even get a free copy of your book and unlimited discount copies.

In twelve short months, we've published more than three-hundred books, compared to the major publishing houses which only add an average of six new titles per year. We will publish your fiction, or non-fiction books about anything, and look forward to reading your stories and sharing them with the world.

We sincerely hope that you will join the growing Starry Night Publishing family, become a published author and gain the world-wide exposure that you deserve. You deserve to succeed. Success comes to those who make opportunities happen, not those who wait for opportunities to happen. You just have to try. Thanks for joining in our journey.

www.starrynightpublishing.com

www.facebook.com/starrynightpublishing/